JOURNAL FOR THE STUDY OF THE OLD TESTAMENT SUPPLEMENT SERIES
159

JSOT Press
Sheffield

The Shape and Shaping of the Psalter

edited by
J. Clinton McCann

Journal for the Study of the Old Testament
Supplement Series 159

Copyright © 1993 Sheffield Academic Press

Published by JSOT Press
JSOT Press is an imprint of
Sheffield Academic Press Ltd
343 Fulwood Road
Sheffield S10 3BP
England

Typeset by Sheffield Academic Press
and
Printed on acid-free paper in Great Britain
by Biddles Limited
Guildford

British Library Cataloguing in Publication Data

A catalogue record for this book is available
from the British Library

ISBN 1-85075-396-2

CONTENTS

PREFACE

As the essays in this volume indicate, there is growing interest among scholars in attempting to understand the book of Psalms not only as a collection of liturgical materials from ancient Israel and Judah but also as a coherent literary whole. Increasingly scholars are discerning and documenting evidence of editorial activity within the Psalter. The purposeful placement of psalms within the collection seems to have given the final form of the whole Psalter a function and message greater than the sum of its parts.

In 1989, a new program unit of the Society of Biblical Literature was formed to contribute to the discussion of the shape and shaping of the Psalter. Seven of the nine essays in this volume were originally presented in sessions of the SBL Psalms Group. James L. Mays's presentation, 'The Question of Context in Psalm Interpretation', opened the inaugural session of the Psalms Group at the 1989 SBL Annual Meeting. In his essay, Mays poses the question of whether attention to the shape and shaping of the Psalter may 'represent a useful third way to go about the critical interpretation of the Psalms'. While not desiring to abandon the traditional form-critical and cult-functional approaches to the Psalter, Mays's own answer to his question is a modest 'yes'. He offers five kinds of data to which interpreters are invited to attend in order to discern the significance of the final form and function of the book of Psalms.

The following essays by Roland E. Murphy and Walter Brueggemann were written and originally presented as direct responses to Mays. Both Murphy and Brueggemann cite the need for caution, and they attempt to provide clarification of Mays's proposal. Murphy's critique, which is presented as a series of six theses, focuses on the need to maintain a firm historical grounding as a criterion for preventing contextual interpretations from becoming arbitrary. Brueggemann evaluates Mays's five kinds of data point by point. He then offers six observations of his own as 'a way to see the Psalter whole'; he concludes from his analysis that 'we are permitted to see the Psalms as a dramatic struggle from obedience (Psalm 1) through dismay (Psalm 73 after 72) to praise (Psalm 150)'.

Gerald Wilson's essay, 'Understanding the Purposeful Arrangement of Psalms in the Psalter: Pitfalls and Promise', was also originally presented at the 1989 SBL Annual Meeting. While not directly responding to Mays, Wilson addresses the same basic issue. After evaluating several recent attempts to discern editorial purpose in various books of the Psalter or the Psalter as a whole, Wilson concludes 'that any progress in understanding the purposeful arrangement of the psalms in the Psalter must begin... with a detailed and careful analysis of the linguistic, literary and thematic linkages that can be discerned among the psalms'.

The first four essays in Part I of this volume are perhaps sufficient to suggest, in response to Mays's question, that scholarly investigation of the shape and shaping of the Psalter is already 'a useful third way to go about critical interpretation of the Psalms'. Further evidence in this regard is provided by the final essay in Part I by David M. Howard, Jr, 'Editorial Activity in the Psalter: A State-of-the-Field Survey'. Originally published in 1989 in the journal *Word and World*, Howard's essay has been revised slightly to reflect scholarly work into 1991. His extensive survey and the bibliographic information in his notes provide an excellent starting point from which to become familiar with recent and current scholarly work on the shape and shaping of the Psalter.

In his discussion of editorial activity in the Psalter, Howard distinguishes between the higher level of concern over the final form of the Psalter and the lower level of interest in relationships between psalms and among groupings of psalms. This distinction prepares the reader for Part II of this volume, which consists of four essays that illustrate both the higher and lower levels of concern with the shaping of the Psalter. In the first essay in Part II, 'Shaping the Psalter: A Consideration of Editorial Linkage in the Book of Psalms', Gerald H. Wilson demonstrates the highest level of concern. He is interested not only in the shapes of the individual books of the Psalter, but also the way in which the five books have been linked together to form the whole Psalter. In building upon and extending the groundbreaking work embodied in his 1985 volume, *The Editing of the Hebrew Psalter*, Wilson offers the conclusion that 'the shape of the canonical Psalter preserves a tense dialogue (or a dialogue in tension) between the royal covenantal hopes associated with the first two-thirds of the Psalter [Psalms 1–89] and the wisdom counsel to trust YHWH alone associated with the final third [Psalms 90–150]'. Wilson's essay was originally presented at the 1990 SBL Annual Meeting.

The final three essays in Part II are more narrowly focused. In 'The Beginning of the Psalter', Patrick D. Miller, Jr begins with a description of the introductory function of Psalms 1 and 2, and then moves to a consideration of the literary and thematic links between Psalms 1–2 and Psalms 3–10. This lower level of interest moves toward the higher level of concern as Miller suggests that Psalms 1–10 (but especially Psalms 1–2) provide a fitting introduction to Book I and to the Psalter as a whole.

In 'Books I–III and the Editorial Purpose of the Hebrew Psalter', J. Clinton McCann, Jr starts with Wilson's observation on the importance of psalms placed at the 'seams' of the Psalter. In contrast to Wilson who calls attention to the psalms at the ends of Books I–III (Psalms 41, 72, 89), McCann focuses on the psalms at the beginning of Books I–III (Psalms 1–2, 42–44, 73–74). In McCann's view, lower level work in detecting links between psalms at the beginnings of Books I–III lends support to Wilson's higher level conclusion about the editorial purpose of the Psalter. McCann's essay was originally presented at the 1990 SBL Annual Meeting.

In 'A Contextual Reading of Psalms 90–94', David M. Howard, Jr demonstrates detailed work on the lower level. He finds significant lexical links 'between every consecutive psalm in Psalms 90–94, and between many non-adjacent psalms as well'. His findings have implications for understanding the larger structure and function of Book IV (Psalms 90–106). Howard's essay was originally presented at the 1990 SBL Annual Meeting.

It should be noted that investigation of the shape and shaping of the Psalter is continuing and that several scholars have begun to explore further the theological implications of the conclusions of this new approach. For instance, the April, 1992 issue of the journal *Interpretation* (Volume 46.2) is devoted to the book of Psalms. It contains four essays which address the theological significance of the Psalms, three of which proceed by taking seriously the shape and shaping of the Psalter (J. Clinton McCann, Jr, 'The Psalms as Instruction', pp. 117-28; Gerald H. Wilson, 'The Shape of the Book of Psalms', pp. 129-42 and Gerald T. Sheppard, 'Theology and the Book of Psalms', pp. 143-55).

I express my deep appreciation to those who have co-operated with me in the production of this volume by contributing their essays. Thanks also to the staff and Program Committee of the SBL for facilitating our work and its presentation; to the members of the Steering Committee of the SBL Psalms Group for their ongoing work in support of Psalms research (Murray Haar, Maribeth Howell, OP, Elizabeth F. Huwiler, John S. Kselman, J. Kenneth Kuntz, James Limburg, Patrick D. Miller, Jr, Irene Nowell, OP, Stephen B. Reid); to David Gunn and David J.A. Clines of the JSOT Press for the conversations which led to the commitment to publish this volume; to the editors of *Word and World* for permission to reprint 'Editorial Activity in the Psalter: A State-of-the Field Survey' by David M. Howard, Jr and to Mary Swehla, Eden faculty secretary, for her careful and conscientious attention to the preparation of the manuscript.

I wish to dedicate my portion of the work on this volume to James L. Mays and Roland E. Murphy, O. Carm., whose wisdom and faithfulness continue to inspire and guide me and a multitude of their students, colleagues and readers.

J. Clinton McCann, Jr
Webster Groves, MO

ABBREVIATIONS

AB	Anchor Bible
Bib	*Biblica*
BHS	*Biblia hebraica stuttgartensia*
BTB	*Biblical Theology Bulletin*
BKAT	Biblischer Kommentar: Altes Testament
BZAW	Beihefte zur *ZAW*
CBQ	*Catholic Biblical Quarterly*
FOTL	The Forms of Old Testament Literature
HAR	*Hebrew Annual Review*
HAT	Handbuch zum Alten Testament
Int	*Interpretation*
JBL	*Journal of Biblical Literature*
JETS	*Journal of the Evangelical Theological Society*
JSOT	*Journal for the Study of the Old Testament*
JSOTSup	*Journal for the Study of the Old Testament*, Supplement Series
JSS	*Journal of Semitic Studies*
JTS	*Journal of Theological Studies*
OBO	Orbis biblicus et orientalis
OTL	Old Testament Library
SBL	Society of Biblical Literature
SBLDS	SBL Dissertation Series
SBLMS	SBL Monograph Series
SBS	Stuttgarter Bibelstudien
Sem	*Semitica*
TOTC	Tyndale Old Testament Commentaries
TZ	*Theologische Zeitschrift*
VT	*Vetus Testamentum*
VTSup	*Vetus Testamentum*, Supplements
WA	M. Luther, *Kritische Gesamtausgabe*(='Weimar edition')
WBC	Word Biblical Commentary
ZAW	*Zeitschrift für die alttestamentliche Wissenschaft*

CONTRIBUTORS

Walter Brueggemann
Columbia Theological Seminary, Decatur, GA

David M. Howard, Jr
Trinity Evangelical Divinity School, Deerfield, IL

J. Clinton McCann, Jr
Eden Theological Seminary, Webster Groves, MO

James Luther Mays
Union Theological Seminary in Virginia, Richmond, VA

Patrick D. Miller
Princeton Theological Seminary, NJ

Roland E. Murphy, O. Carm.
Duke University, Washington, DC

Gerald H. Wilson
Newberg, OR

Part I

A NEW APPROACH TO THE PSALTER

THE QUESTION OF CONTEXT IN PSALM INTERPRETATION

James L. Mays

Is it possible and useful to read a psalm as part of the book of Psalms, to understand it under the directives furnished by the book as a whole, to interpret its language by the context established by the piety and thinking inferred from the psalms in the book in their relation to each other? Or, to put it another way, can the mentality that turned the collection of cultic pieces into literature be educed in sufficient specificity to provide a guide to the way the psalms were being understood and composed, a kind of *geistige Heimat* of the Psalter in its final stage of formation?

The possibility of deriving a context for interpretation from the book is not raised as a substitute for the dominant approaches in current Psalms study. In the standard commentaries and introductions, psalms are taken up individually and identified as an instance of a genre, and/or as agenda for ritual performance, or as artefacts of Israel's religious history in the context of the ancient Near East. The context for construal is an ideal genre and its proposed history, an inferred festival or ritual occasion, or the ancient Near Eastern history of religion. These approaches have been enormously clarifying and productive. It will be impossible to develop a description of the character of the psalms apart from what has been learned through them.

Of course, the difficulties that arise in giving psalms interpretive identity and context are well known—the tension between the actuality of so many psalms and the ideal *Gattung* to which they are assigned, the unresolved questions of cultic history, the perplexing problem of the identity of the individual, the effect on meaning of moving traditional forms and words into quite different periods of religious history and the extent of redaction in the Psalter. All reckon with the fact that the Psalter is the result of a long history. As the career of Israel passed through dramatic changes, the givens of the settings of earlier psalms changed. Traditional patterns and vocabularies took on modified significance and roles. Older psalms were reinterpreted to fit new conditions, and new psalms were written in continuity with classic conventions, but expressing the needs and thoughts of later times. Because of the importance of this history for the actuality of its outcome, it seems an anomaly that the Psalter itself is generally so little considered to be significant as an interpretive context. It represents after all the one given context from which to seek guidance about how the language of particular psalms is to be understood.

There are signs in Psalms study that this anomaly is recognized and is being addressed in various ways. Among those that I have found particularly helpful are: Gerald Wilson's fresh assault on the question of the ordering of the psalms;[1] Joichim Becker's study of Israel's rereading and reinterpretation of the psalms;[2] Fritz Stolz's description of what he calls the post-cultic milieu in which psalms were composed after the Exile;[3] a number of studies of the redaction of individual psalms[4] and the quite different treatments in the introductions of Brevard Childs and Klaus Seybold.[5] In 'The Place of the Torah-Psalms in the Psalter',[6] I attempted to gain some purchase on the question. The paper seeks to discover the relation of Psalms 1, 19, and 119 to the book of Psalms. It concludes that this trio, rather than being an odd addendum, stands in a fabric of relations to other psalms and

---

1.   G. Wilson, *The Editing of the Hebrew Psalter* (SBLDS, 76; Chico, CA: Scholars Press, 1985); 'Evidence of Editorial Divisions in the Hebrew Psalter', *VT* 34 (1984), pp. 337-52; 'The Use of "Untitled" Psalms in the Hebrew Psalter', *ZAW* 97 (1985), pp. 404-13; 'The Use of Royal Psalms at the "Seams" of the Hebrew Psalter', *JSOT* 35 (1986), pp. 85-94.

2.   J. Becker, *Israel deutet seine Psalmen: Urform und Neuinterpretation in den Psalmen* (SBS, 18; Stuttgart: Katholisches Bibelwerk, 1966).

3.   F. Stolz, *Psalmen im nachkultischen Raum* (Theologische Studien, 129; Zurich: Theologischen Verlag, 1983).

4.   T. Veijola, *Verneissung in der Krise: Studien zur Literatur und Theologie der Exilszeit anhand des 89. Psalms* (Helsinki: Suomalainen Tiedeakatemia, 1982); W. Beyerlin, *Werden und Wesen des 107. Psalms* (BZAW, 153; Berlin: W. de Gruyter, 1978).

5.   B.S. Childs, *Introduction to the Old Testament as Scripture* (Philadelphia: Fortress Press, 1979); K. Seybold, *Introducing the Psalms* (trans. R.G. Dunphy; Edinburgh: T. & T. Clark , 1990).

6.   J.L. Mays, 'The Place of the Torah-Psalms in the Psalter', *JBL* 106/1 (1987), pp. 3-12.

to the whole that gives insight into the terms in which the whole was read, and for describing the piety that sponsored and was nurtured by the Psalter. Strategic as they are for the problem, these three psalms provide only one entry. The net must be cast more widely.

To what kind of data should one look to derive a picture of a context for reading psalms as part of the book? The Psalter seems so patently a collection that the task is discouraging. The framework and integrating redaction to be found in books like Genesis or Judges is not evident in the Psalter. The problem is more like that of a book like Amos, where one deals also with an assembly of units. Yet in contrast to Amos, the Psalter seems to contain quite individual and distinct pieces whose relation to each other is not a feature of their being in the book, but rather of sharing a type or function.

I want to propose five kinds of data that can be used to construct a description of the understanding, mentality and piety that led to and used the book of Psalms. For each kind of data, I will point to a few illustrations of what is in mind. I realize that by referring briefly to a selection of psalms whose character I judge to be illustrative I am begging all sorts of exegetical questions. The illustrations are to be taken simply as pointers to make clear what is in mind and as a way of making the question more specific for the respondents to this essay.

1. *An Interpretive Ordering of the Psalms*

This is the first and obvious consideration that comes to mind, since it is a matter of the book as a whole. Because of the way the book was built, it may not be possible to account for the location and contiguous relations of every psalm in terms of an intentional scheme, but over-arching and organizing patterns which point to what the arrangers had in mind have been identified.

The Psalter has an introduction. Psalms 1 and 2 together elevate the paired topics of Torah and kingship of the Lord. This introduction opens a book which with its five sections is itself a kind of Torah. It introduces themes that occupy much of the book—the questions of how individual life and historical destiny are to turn out, the polarity of the wicked and righteous, and the polarity of Zion and messiah and people of God versus the nations.

The announcement of Psalm 2 of the authority of the messiah over the nations has a counterpart in Psalm 89 at the end of Book III in the great lament over the frustration of the promise to the messianic Davidic king. After transitions in 90–92, the hymns of the coming kingdom of God in 93–100 follow to put the topics in a prophetic–eschatological perspective.

The prayers of David in Books I and II, accompanied by the songs of the official singer-guilds, Asaph and Korah, in Books II and III put the authority of these names and traditions they stand for behind the special identity and use of the Psalter.

The attempt to discern and describe the shape of the Psalter, however, does not reach to all the clues provided by individual psalms. Psalmody began in the festivals and rituals of Israel during the era of the kingdoms, if not earlier. It reached its culmination in the formation of the Psalter, though, I believe, without losing its life and function as the provision of liturgical resources for the worship, prayer and meditation of the people. The crucial psalms for our purpose are those whose redaction or composition reflect the process of movement through stages of cultic history toward the formation of the book. What is needed is to look at these psalms with questions about their implications for views of the whole and for the psalms in it. What features can be identified that point to the way in which all the collected psalms are being understood and used? The context sought, then, is not simply a literary entity; it is also the theological–historical perspective of the mentality that led to the book's formation. So I turn to indications of psalmody's movement toward the double identity of liturgy and literature that belongs to the book of Psalms.

2. A Shift in the Conception and Use of the Genres

Psalm 30 shows how the shift in the conception and use of genres involves a loosening of the constraints of the genre on function and its employment in literary and figurative ways. Psalm 30 belongs to one of the classic types. It is a song of thanksgiving for an individual, but its title identifies it as a 'Psalm for the dedication of the temple'. The individual psalm is designated for corporate use; the report of experience in the psalm now refers to the deliverance of the people from exile. This editorial reclassification is not just evidence of the re-reading of one psalm. It may be evidence of the way first-person psalms were being used and composed. The individual lament has become, by way of Jeremiah and Deutero-Isaiah, a paradigm for understanding and articulating the congregation's experience.

Psalm 129 is a corporate pilgrimage psalm, composed in the style of an individual's lament and prayer. Whether the final form is the result of redaction, or more likely an original composition, it shows the literary and figurative use being made of the type.

Psalm 51 is composed in the style of an individual's penitential prayer, but it has elements that show its corporate use, and motifs and language that reflect prophetic hope for the regeneration of the people. Its title connects it with a narrative about David and renders his experience a midrashic type for that of the nation.

3. *From Ritual Accompaniment to Instruction*

Psalm 33 is an example of the move of psalmody from the primary function of accompaniment towards an increasing expansion of the potential for instruction in all types of psalms. Psalm 33 is a hymn composed with a clear intent to instruct. Comparing it with hymns like 29 or 47 discloses the character of the shift. These first two focus attention on a performance in the cult, while in the case of Psalm 33, attention is focused on the performance of the hymn. It has become the cultic event of significance. All psalms have a pedagogical potential because they say things about God, world and self. The move in some psalms brings that potential into prominence in all the collected psalms.

Psalm 32 is a penitential psalm written to lead and instruct in the practice of penitence.

In Psalm 24, a catechism (vv. 3-6) on qualifications for entering the sanctuary stands between the little hymn (vv. 1-2) and a liturgy of the entrance of the ark into the temple (vv. 7-10). The catechism centers the other two elements on the topic of the moral character of one's relation to the king of the universe. The unity of the text lies in thought rather than an agenda of ritual.

These and other instances of the developing instructional intent suggest that the groups of psalms usually classified as Wisdom and Torah psalms are not a different kind of species from the rest, but stand in continuity with a long and developing tendency.

4. *The Combination and Consolidation of Genres, Topics and Motifs*

Psalms 19 and 119 are, of course, parade examples. Psalm 19 combines three topics and styles in a unity. Psalm 119 is a veritable montage of genres and topics. They are an earnest that combinations of various kinds are pervasive in the Psalter through composition, redaction and pairing. Psalms 136 and 145 combine the divine work of creation and providence with the works of salvation history in praise of God's marvelous deeds. Psalms 103 and 104 are connected as a pair by the unique incipit, 'Bless the Lord, O my soul'. The first is a composition on the topic of the Lord's *ḥesed* in dealing with sinners, and the second is a composition on the topic of God's wisdom in creation and providence in dealing with creatures. The eschatological hymn that concludes Psalm 22 is an ending that raises the import and setting of the preceding individual prayer to a universal level.

5. *Psalms in Reference to Books of Scripture*

Psalms 105 and 106 are versions of the foundational story of Israel, reflecting its linearized and fixed form. Psalm 136 elaborates its praise of the Creator-Savior by use of Genesis 1 (vv. 6-9), Exodus 14 (vv. 13-15) and Numbers 21 (vv. 17-22). Psalm 118 quotes Exodus 15 (v. 14—Exod. 15.2) and 103 quotes Exodus 34 (v. 8—Exod. 34.6) to signal its hermeneutical horizon. And of course, there is the process of attributing psalms to biblical worthies and connecting some with narratives in the books of Samuel.

These, then, are five kinds of data that are features of psalmody on the way toward the book. The idea is that they could be used to elaborate and fill out the clues gained from looking at the structure of the book. They are part of the literary character of the book because they are in it. They provide a guide to the way other psalms to which they are related in various ways were being understood as the book emerged. The project would be to build up a picture of psalmody, a description of the mentality that created the book, to be used as a heuristic context to suggest questions and possibilities for interpreting the Psalms.

When the Psalms are examined from this perspective, questions and possibilities do appear which are not visible when the classic genres and the pre-exilic cult are used as the primary and organizing context. Interest is shifted toward rhetorical structures, and the intra-textual relations of the language of particular psalms with other psalms and with texts in other books of Scripture. Features of the psalm that were anomalies for other contexts find explanation. The horizons for the text are now the great topics and themes and experiences recorded in Scripture.

The question of who says the psalms receives an open and variable answer that corresponds to the way they were being understood and used. Their functions are opened up to a variety of uses for prayer, praise and study that reflect their role as both liturgy and Scripture.

But is such a project possible? Does it represent a useful third way to go about the critical interpretation of the Psalms? Can the character of the book as constituted by such features be described in a way adequate to serve as a context for understanding the collected poems in their identity as a 'psalm' and as a guide to the mentality and piety that created and used the Psalter?

REFLECTIONS ON CONTEXTUAL INTERPRETATION OF THE PSALMS

Roland E. Murphy, O. Carm.

In biblical studies it is almost unheard of that exegesis should operate without the context of the book in which a passage is found. In the past, exceptions were made for psalms and proverbs; these were considered to be independent compositions with little, if any, relationship to the 'book' in which they were found. Slowly this has changed and the 'independence' of the proverbial sayings has yielded to the recognition of *mots crochets*, and other binding phenomena. Long ago it was recognized that there was a common *Formensprache* in the vocabulary and phraseology of the psalms, but the context was sought in historical circumstances rather than in linguistic or literary phenomena. The question of contextual interpretation of the Psalter has risen to a new level. As Professor Mays has asked: 'Is it possible and useful to read a psalm as part of the book of Psalms, to understand it under the directives furnished by the book as a whole?' I would like to answer the question in terms of the following theses.

Thesis 1

Hypothetical historical reconstruction is as inescapable in contextual interpretation as it is in the usual historical criticism that is applied to the Psalter. This is a cautionary observation, lest the new contextual studies of the Psalter in the context of canon or book might seem more 'objective' than other approaches.

The point can be illustrated briefly. We are all acquainted with the hypotheses that lurk behind the approach of Gunkel, or Mowinckel or other practitioners of historical criticism (for example, hypotheses about the original *Sitz im Leben*). What hypotheses lurk behind the reading of a psalm within the context of a book? The first is the nature of the 'book'. It has been divided into five books, so there is a prehistory to the book—the gradual collection of groups of psalms and the eventual amalgamation of these groups to form the Psalter. We recognize the five books (and the consequent analogy with the Torah, which is read into this division). Then we move into the pre-history of this collection—the gradual grouping of psalms, such as Davidic, Asaphite, Korahite or songs of ascents and the eventual formation within the Psalter as it stands. Each one of these steps constitutes a kind of context; for example the figure of David as a key to the Davidic psalms; the pilgrimage to the holy city for the psalms of ascents, and so forth. Two observations that I make are that first these and many other divisions of groups within the Psalter are historical reconstructions, and secondly, they have a certain context that bonds them and creates a hermeneutical key; this may yield by being subsumed into a larger unit much as, say, the thrust of the Priestly material is muted within the overall message of the Pentateuch. The unity of the Psalter is not unlike the disunity of the Torah, in terms of its pre-history. There were undoubtedly several contexts for the individual collections, and for the Psalter as a whole we are challenged by a new context, created by the establishment of a cut-off point at 150.

Moreover, there is considerable reconstruction in the interpretation of certain of the psalms within the book. A parade example would be the function attributed to the first two psalms. Together, these psalms according to Mays, 'elevate the paired topics of Torah and kingship of the Lord. This introduction opens a book which with its five sections is itself a kind of Torah. It introduces themes that occupy much of the book—the questions of how individual life and historical destiny are to turn out, the polarity of the wicked and righteous, and the polarity of Zion and messiah and people of God versus the nations'. Psalm 1, it must be confessed, is an anomaly. It is not a prayer, it is a blessing upon those who go the right way, in contrast to those who do not. In the words of Klaus Seybold: 'The reader of the Psalter is greeted at the outset as a reader of the Law (the *Torah*), and is admonished. This no doubt presupposes that the book in the hand of this reader already belongs to the Holy Writings which make up the third part of the Hebrew canon, after the "Law" and the "Prophets"'.[1] I find this reasonable, just as I find many a hypothesis reasonable. But I am not willing

---

1.   K. Seybold, *Introducing the Psalms* (trans. R.G. Dunphy; Edinburgh: T. & T. Clark, 1990), p. 15. He goes on to say that Psalm 1 is both a foreword and a motto for what follows.

to go further and associate Psalm 2 with Psalm 1, as Mays has done. Other points binding Psalms 1–2 can be added—Psalm 2 ends with a blessing (2.12b), forming an inclusion with 1.1; in addition the closing verses (1.6, 2.12) both speak of a way that perishes.[1] How is one to evaluate these reasons? One can indulge in more speculation. For example, the ending of 2.12 proclaims 'happy are all who take refuge in him' (referring to God). Who are these 'all' if not those whose faith emulates David, of whom the psalm says, 'You are my son'? Thus Psalm 2 becomes a fitting introduction to the Davidic psalter in Psalms 3–41 (if not 3–72!).[2] Or to complicate the implications of these hints, one can point out that there is an echo of Ps. 2.1 in Ps. 89.51: 'Why do the nations rage...?' (2.1) and the request of the psalmist 'Remember, O Lord, the insults to your servants...all the accusations of the nations' (89.51).[3] Notice that I am not denying that these are insightful comments, I am merely saying that they all partake of a hypothetical character; one can associate freely between one psalm and another in the context of a book. The associations hardly justify a solid context from which to draw conclusions.

Thesis 2

The book 'context' of a psalm may not be as stirring, as spiritually attractive as another equally valid context (the historical for example); its value may be very limited. I would agree with Mays that it is 'possible and useful to read a psalm as part of the book of Psalms', in other words, to give to a specific psalm the context of a book to which it belongs, but I think that its usefulness would be relatively limited. Psalm 30 can serve as an example. This, it will be remembered, is a parade example of a thanksgiving hymn: 'I cried out to you and you healed me...You brought me up from Sheol' (vv. 2-3). The superscription designates it as a 'Psalm for the dedication of the temple'. Whether this refers to the second temple (515) or the feast of Hanukkah is

---

1. In *Introducing the Psalms*, p. 126, Seybold distinguishes between Psalms 1 and 2; the first is 'a didactic Wisdom Poem of late postexilic origin'; the second is 'an old royal text from the pre-exilic period'. But even if they are different (as a motto is from an introduction), Psalm 1 serves to frame Psalms 2 and following, and Psalm 2 introduces the series of 2–72 (even Psalm 89).

2. Seybold, *Introducing the Psalms*, pp. 146-47.

3. So Seybold, *Introducing the Psalms*, p. 26.

irrelevant. The point is that the psalm, as Mays phrases it, 'is designated for corporate use; the report of experience in the psalm now refers to the deliverance of the people from the exile'. Assuming this new context as a concrete situation in which the psalm was re-used, is it a real gain? Only very minor, it seems to me. It is 'editorial reclassification' and perhaps it 'points to the way first-person psalms were being used and composed' (Mays). Perhaps the times called for that. But I think this new *Sitz im Leben* rather cuts off a psalm that has a greater potential for application. Is the new context better than the one originally established by historical criticism? I doubt it. The historical interpretation also involved the community in the rejoicing and praise of the individual (30.5). It seems somewhat artificial to blow the psalm up to a community experience of resurrection from exilic death in the style of Ezekiel 37. In this respect I should not be too quick to claim one level of meaning for the literal historical sense. The original *Sitz im Leben* of this psalm, according to E. Gerstenberger, would have been the response to a healing ritual, which only later was transferred from the small group or family to congregational worship and eventually to the temple.[1]

Thesis 3

There is a relationship between worship and teaching. How is this to be construed in the Psalter? Mays describes this aspect as 'the move of psalmody from the primary function of ritual accompaniment toward an increasing expansion of the instructional potential in all types of psalms'. Perhaps this move was already implicit in the traditional genre of thanksgiving. One of the component parts of the thanksgiving hymn is the *Bekenntnis* or testimony in which the person who has experienced a deliverance gives witness to it.[2] Thus in Psalm 30 there is the lesson that the Lord's anger is only for a moment, but God's favor is for a lifetime (30.6). The psalmist tells bystanders that those who look to God will be radiant, the lowly are heard by the Lord when they call out (34.6-7). The instructional element was in the thanksgiving psalm from the beginning, insofar as the psalmist was

1.   E. Gerstenberger, *Psalms: Part I* (FOTL, 14; Grand Rapids: Eerdmans, 1988), p. 135.
2.   Cf. R.E. Murphy, 'A Consideration of the Classification "Wisdom Psalms"' (VTSup, 9; Leiden: Brill, 1962), pp. 156-67 (163, 167).

spurred to encourage others to share in the experience. If the move here is to focus attention on the 'performance of the hymn' (so Mays), it is a natural outgrowth of the mood of thanksgiving.

The 'performance' of a psalm, focusing on the prayer itself and not on its place in the cult, is due to what James Kugel has called the 'Scripturalization' of the Psalms:

> For as the Psalms became Scripture, they did so with an interpretive strategy attached: they were not to be interpreted as a self-standing book of prayers or praises, any more than Proverbs was to be a self-standing collection of wise sayings. Both were adjuncts to the rest of Scripture, to be read in the light of other books, to be interpreted and studied, in at least some cases to be connected to incidents in the narrated lives of their alleged authors—and *hence*, not wholly sufficient for the congregation's (or individual's) needs in worship.[1]

He goes on to distinguish between the Psalms-as-text-for-teaching (that is from God to human) and Psalms-as-text-for-worship (from human to God). One can see here at work the line from Psalm 1, 'studying the teaching day and night' (v. 2).

Thesis 4

This thesis is triggered by the words of Martin Luther, and it is that a theological or emotive context engendered by the Psalms can ensure an adequate understanding. Here the context is generated by an intense personal reading of the psalm that is appropriated by the reader. The words of Luther are as follows:

> None can pray a psalm if they have not previously made the words of the psalm their own. But they will then be your own when you have the same feeling and the same spirit in which the words were said. If you pray without this, you resemble those who play a role in a comedy, where the action takes place with proper words, but with a reality that is artificial. What a shipwrecked person really says sounds quite different coming from the actor who plays the part of the shipwrecked, or a mask, even though the words remain the same. For the former speaks his own words, the latter speaks words that are foreign, and naturally with a different feeling. For the former, reality and words cohere; for the latter, reality is simulated.[2]

---

1.   J.L. Kugel, 'Topics in the History of the Spirituality of the Psalms', in A. Green (ed.), *Jewish Spirituality from the Bible through the Middle Ages* (World Spirituality, 13; New York: Crossroad, 1986), p. 136.
2.   I translate from the German translation of the scholion for Psalm 5, since I

This thesis can be understood on a pre-critical level or on a sophisticated critical level. Perhaps the best example is the frequent near encounter or actual encounter with death/Sheol in the Psalms. It is an astonishing fact that many Christians have been consoled in their struggle with death by psalms which contain no proclamation of victory over death.[1] How is that possible? The theologically unsophisticated person is in a context of struggling with real physical death and it is colored by his or her belief in immortality. The restoration to life which the psalmists so often celebrate can be understood on the level of eternal life, and so it often is to the great consolation of the one who prays. The reader has captured the feeling and spirit of the psalm and made that personal to self, even if on a transcendent plane. Life is life! And the struggle for life goes on, on many levels. Perhaps the proper characterization of this context is 'reader-response'. That is where the reader is, and the reader is truly assimilating the message of the psalm on a level that is meaningful, without being distorting.

Thesis 5

Some criteria have to be forged in order to weed out unprofitable or even erroneous contextualizations. This is essentially a negative point,

---

was not able to find the original Latin. The text is in *Martin Luther: Die reformatorischen Grundschriften in vier Bänden*, in H. Beintker (ed.), *Reform von Theologie, Kirche und Gesellschaft* (Munich: Deutscher Taschenbuch Verlag, 1983), II, p. 25. Beintker points out (p. 147) the interesting fact that a small portion of Luther's explanation of Psalm 5 (v. 12) was known and published in his Works (*WA* I, pp. 347ff.) as 'Fragmentum Lectionum Lutheri'. Then an extensive Latin fragment of Psalms 4 and 5 was discovered in the Vatican, but it was judged to be merely a student's notes on Luther's lecture. More exact examination showed that it was indeed an example of Luther's exegesis, from the year 1516 and perhaps 1517. The Latin original was published in *WA* 55II, and also in Vol. I of the *Archiv zur Weimarer Ausgabe der Werke Martin Luthers: Texte und Untersuchungen* (*Cologne*, pp. 1981 ff.).

1. The point has been expressed well by C. Barth: 'In his famous introduction to the psalms, H. Gunkel says of the individual psalms of lamentation that they are "the place where the religion of the psalms comes into conflict with death". In a less well-known comment, O. Noordmans says of this conflict that the psalms are the greatest of all the wonders of the world; for without giving any clear knowledge of the nature of death, "they have helped one generation after another to pass through death"'. See *Introduction to the Psalms* (New York: Charles Scribner's Sons, 1966), p. 49.

a kind of brake on untrammelled reader response. One general criterion would be, does the context limit or contract the open-endedness of the psalm? Here I think of Davidic authorship, with the specifics as to the particular situation he was in when he 'wrote' the psalm (some thirteen psalms). This is inhibiting and thus not a helpful context. It keys into a particular event in the life of David that has only a very extrinsic connection with the psalm, and often enough is misleading. In any case, it points to David more than to a universal human experience. There is a lesson here from Brevard Childs's handling of the Davidic authorship. In effect he allows the figure of David to evaporate and in David's stead emerges Everyman:

> Psalms which once functioned within a cult context were historicized by placing them within the history of David...David is pictured as a man...He emerges as a person who experiences the full range of human emotions...The effect of this new context has wide hermeneutical implications. The psalms are transmitted as the sacred psalms of David, but they testify to all the common troubles and joys of ordinary human life in which all persons participate.[1]

Thesis 6

There are several contexts in which the Bible is read. What is desirable, even necessary, is a certain continuity between contexts. Professor Mays does not advocate a contextual interpretation as a substitute for other approaches. He would recognize various other contexts as well as that of the 'book' which he has proposed for discussion. What my thesis proposes is that with the pluriformity of contexts, some kind of criterion is called for if interpretation is not to be anarchy. The criterion I would propose is continuity—there should be some kind of continuity existing between the literal historical sense and the various meanings. This criterion should function both positively and negatively. It should point in a direction, and it should serve to eliminate arbitrary proposals. Perhaps the thesis should be kept as general as it is written.

---

1. Cf. B.S. Childs, *Introduction to the Old Testament as Scripture* (Philadelphia: Fortress Press, 1979), p. 521. My preference, of all the superscriptions in the psalms is 102.1, 'The prayer of an afflicted one when he is faint and pours out his plea before the Lord'. This captures the mood of vv. 2-12. Perhaps it was adapted for community use by the *relecture* in vv. 13-29?

The need for some kind of thesis such as this can perhaps be illustrated in a scale of possible contextual interpretations: possible oral stage; fixation in writing with possible retouches all along the way; association with other groups of psalms by authorship (David, Asaph, etc.) or by subject matter (songs of ascents); pre-exilic or postexilic situations; the additions of the titles to the psalms; the context of Qumran; of the New Testament; of the rabbis; of the early, medieval, and Reformation church and the modern approach of historical criticism. It almost appears as if there is no end to contextual interpretations. Are they all to be accepted as they stand? Criteria have to be worked out for evaluation of various contexts. I would be in favor of the historical literal meaning as the basic norm, and criterion guide. I think that this would also apply to the 'book' context that we have been discussing.

RESPONSE TO JAMES L. MAYS, 'THE QUESTION OF CONTEXT'

Walter Brueggemann

Professor Mays has articulated for us questions that are both important and difficult. The questions he raises are important because it is clear that we are at the threshold of a quite new season in Psalm studies. The work rooted in Gunkel and Mowinckel is exceedingly important and, as Mays indicates, not to be abandoned. That work however, foundational as it is, is no longer an adequate basis from which to consider our current situation in scholarship.

The questions Mays articulates are difficult because we are only at the threshold. The categories in which we should proceed are not clear or agreed upon. Indeed Mays's own question is whether the new venture of scholarship he envisions is even possible. His attempt to answer that question is characteristically concrete and practical. He does not discuss the general or theoretical issue of possibility, but begins to struggle specifically with how an answer might look. My response to the rich suggestion of Mays concerns not only the specifics of his comments, but the larger issue of how cultic texts and types may be understood as leading to the creation of the Psalter as a script for 'torah-piety'. Thus it is the substantive issue of new approaches and not simply Mays's own probe that is the concern of this essay.

I

There are in Mays's paper two sets of questions that are closely related to each other, but are not the same. On the one hand, he is concerned with deriving 'a context for interpretation from the book', and he refers to the ways in which specific psalms stand in a 'fabric of relations to other psalms'. I understand this phrasing to be concerned with the canonical *shape* of the book of Psalms (so Childs), and the questions of how the several parts constitute the whole, and how the reading of the whole is related to the reading of the parts. This concern takes up the question of the 'final form of the text'. I will make a fuller response to this concern in the last part of this essay.

On the other hand, Mays speaks of factors which led to the formation of the book of Psalms. He gives a great deal of attention to this more dynamic phenomenon, and concludes with comments concerning features of psalmody on the way toward the book. At one point he speaks of the 'process of movement... toward the formation of the book'. This much more dynamic phrasing is concerned with the canonical *process* (so Sanders), as distinct from the canonical *shape*. So far as I know, this is a new framing of the question for Mays which I find much more difficult and elusive than the notion of shape, much more speculative, but no less important.

I suggest that canonical shape (context) and canonical process require us to think about two very different matters. The former, context, concerns the relation of the part to the whole. The latter, process, implies that there is a development, presumably traceable, which produced the Psalter. It may be that the second question is the only way to get at the first one, though I shall suggest that this latter notion of developmental process is not without problems (see Section III below).

II

Mays's restlessness with the outcomes of the work of Gunkel and Mowinckel is important for the pursuit of canonical questions, but that restlessness is not peculiar to Mays. In genre analysis, it is widely recognized that the assumptions of scholarship are enormously speculative concerning the proposed history of ideal genre, and tend toward reductionism. The problem of genre analysis is compounded by the fact that in much of scholarship, the notion of genre has been reified so that the specific psalm must submit to the proposed genre.[1]

---

1. This is the classic criticism J. Muilenburg ('Form Criticism and Beyond', *JBL* 88 [1969], pp. 1-28), has made of form criticism. He writes: 'But there has been a proclivity among scholars in recent years to lay such stress upon the typical and representative that the individual, personal and unique features of the particular pericope are all but lost to view... To state our criticism in another way, form criticism by its very nature is bound to generalize because it is concerned with what is common to all the representatives of a genre, and therefore applies an external measure to the individual pericopes. It does not focus sufficient attention upon what

With regard to the widely embraced cultic setting of the Psalms, two criticisms are easily made. First, as Mays recognizes, the cultic setting of the Psalms is notoriously hypothetical. Secondly, whatever may be said about the cultic origin of the Psalms, they are not now Psalms of the temple; if they were, they would by definition be cut off from any continuing contemporaneity for later Judaism. Thus the continued relevance of the Psalms depends on them being freed from any temple context. The literature of the Psalms has become something other than cultic material that is considerably removed from that proposed cultic setting. Therefore the cultic setting of the Psalms is not only speculative, but also places interpretive value on an original setting removed from what we now have in the Psalter.

Mays—like Westermann—is not very explicit about cult, but his unexpressed notion of cult is contrasted with a more didactic or pedagogical function of the Psalms in a less explicit ritual context. This contrast between ritual accompaniment and more instructionally focused usage of the Psalms is important to Mays's proposal. I wonder, however, about a notion of cult other than the one with which Mays operates. I suggest that cult be understood as the 'matrix of symbolization' in which the community continually reasserts its identity and reconstructs its life, for itself and for its young.[1] Every community, if it is not to disintegrate, must engage in such on-going symbolization and re-symbolization.[2] Thus I suggest that in some way, even in a post-exilic, post-temple, or 'post-cultic' context, Israel must still be engaged in intentional communal re-symbolization. Because Mowinckel's cultic claims are undoubtedly overstated, non-cultic alternatives tend to be overstated in parallel responding fashion. However, I doubt whether a critique of Mowinckel requires or even permits a simple, one-dimensional move from cultic to didactic, because I do not think the functions of communities can be so simply and clearly slotted. At the

is unique and unrepeatable, upon the particularity of the formulation' (p. 5).

1.   I have attempted to explicate this notion in *Israel's Praise: Doxology against Idolatry and Ideology* (Philadelphia: Fortress Press, 1988). On the work of the community engaged in symbolization, see P.L. Berger and T. Luckmann, *The Social Construction of Reality* (Garden City, NY: Doubleday, 1967).

2.   'Re-symbolization' means that the act of symbolization is not only repetitive and reiterative, but must be modified and transformed to comprehend new experience and stay pertinent. See Berger and Luckmann, *The Social Construction of Reality*, pp. 153-63.

very least, I suggest 'post-cultic' is a misnomer. Thus I imagine that even after the exile, Psalms are in some sense cultic. Mays's carefully nuanced language tends to soften the distinctions I am pursuing, but the issue is nonetheless an important one, given the history of Psalm interpretation.

III

I suggest that in Mays's proposal there is a powerful Wellhausean presupposition about the history of Israelite religion related to the distinction of cult as context and book as context.[1] Mays's sense of development and movement is from cult to book, from tight genres to loosening of constraints of genre, from ritual function to instructional use. It appears to me that all these various contrasting pairs reflect and assume a contrast between 'Israelite religion' and 'exilic or postexilic Judaism'. I understand Mays's concern to be that the book of Psalms is not a book reflective of 'Israelite religion' but rather reflective of later Judaism. The work of the great critics (especially Mowinckel) attempted to understand the Psalms in relation to Israelite religion of the temple period when in fact the Psalter is a document of postexilic Judaism. It may be that this programmatic distinction is a fruitful one, especially when made explicitly.

The danger may be that our usual assumptions about the development of Israelite religion over-stress the discontinuity of Judaism from earlier Israelite religion; perhaps we bring to the argument assumptions about Judaism that are as unhelpful as the assumptions of Gunkel and Mowinckel. It is clear that the liturgical documents of later Judaism had to make enormous adjustments to deal with the problematic realities of Jewish life in a Persian or Hellenistic environment. I wonder, however, if in the face of this demanding, indispensable adjustment, the classic forms of speech, even with significantly new functions, did not continue to be enormously important, not only pedagogically but in terms of 'world construction'. I wonder, moreover, if these uses were not only 'instructional', but in fact were acts of 're-symbolization' whereby the community kept its identity visible and available. That is, while the modes of symbolization may have been different, the community had an on-going need for just such activity. I would therefore

1. For a recent reassessment of Wellhausen's commanding hypothesis, see *Semeia* 25 (1983).

not want to state too sharply the contrast between earlier and later use of the texts in world-forming cultic activity of the community.

Thus Mays has posed for us two important issues, but they do not easily cohere with each other. On the one hand, the book as context is a literary-canonical question. On the other hand, the question of 'movement' is a historical-critical one. Insofar as the developmental process is a historical-critical issue, interpretation seems to be made with reference to projected historical reality and not to the body of the book itself. That is, Mays's canonical-contextual approach does not escape historical speculation so long as it depends on the classic Wellhausen discontinuity. I suggest that the constructs and categories of historical criticism, or criticism of the history of Israelite religion, loom large for us and do not easily permit us to take the book simply as context. Indeed, I am not sure whether 'book as context' is desirable. But if it is desirable, it is far from obvious how we interpret in that way, without reference to the assumed development of Israelite religion. Thus I believe ambiguity about book as context and history as context runs throughout Mays's paper and is likely to be an on-going problem for us for a long time to come. I wonder if we can have it both ways. In any case, if we are able to opt for one or the other, that is book as context or history as context, our construals of the book of Psalms will be very different.

IV

Mays's specific points are suggestive and deserve careful attention. Taken one at a time, they have enormous heuristic value. Taken together, his points are an odd lot. I take their variation to be an indication not only of the vitality of Mays's thought, but also as a signal that we are only at the beginning of our new work.

1. Mays's first of five points is of a peculiar kind, perhaps his most important category for study. It concerns not the processive move of the Psalter but the shape and context of the Psalter as we have it. This sort of argument is much easier to control than the argument about process, though it may also in the long run be less interesting and less productive for our understanding. I will offer a specific suggestion in this direction at the end of my paper.

2. Concerning the loosening of the constraints of genre on function, Mays suggests that the superscription of Psalm 30 shows that psalm

being put to new use.[1] While I think that is true, Mays's treatment suggests two other issues. First the juxtaposition of superscription ('A Song at the dedication of the temple') and genre is an odd juxtaposition which tends, in my judgment, to treat genre in a rather reified way. The fact that the superscription violates the genre may be a problem for our scholarship. I am not convinced that it entailed such a drastic shift for the psalm-makers who had not read Gunkel. Did the makers of the superscription know that they were dealing with an individual song of thanksgiving, or was it not an individual psalm of thanksgiving until Gunkel made it so? Indeed, v. 5 speaks of the 'saints', suggesting the psalm was never so individual as our genre analysis may have suggested.[2] I wonder if rather than saying this is a movement from one to the other, from a genre of individual song to superscripted temple song, we may say simply that the psalm is richly polyvalent and could seed Israel's imagination in many ways, not only imagination tamed by a genre.

Secondly, Mays has it that the psalm is understood as 'the deliverance of the people from exile'. I find this a rich suggestion; I am, however, hard put to know what sort of comment that is. Since Mays shares none of his reasoning, this does not seem to me to be an exegetical comment from either the text or the superscription, but reflects the exilic dimension of Mays's notion of the process of the formation of the book of Psalms, a notion dependent upon a historical construct.

I wonder if in making this interpretation, Mays is not making excessive use of genre himself in order to show a move outside the genre. It may be preferable to say simply that the text lets itself be heard in different ways. I am not sure that the psalm with its superscription is in fact 'a loosening of the constraints of the genre', or if that is our own post-Gunkel requirement. Behind this question is the question about

---

1.   Mays follows a substantial line of interpreters in noticing the matter of 'new use'. Thus H.-J. Kraus, *Psalms 1–59: A Commentary* (Minneapolis: Augsburg, 1988), p. 354, writes that Psalm 30, 'has therefore been transferred from individual experience to the community and its worship'. On Kraus's own exegesis, however, the transference is before the psalm was composed, because in its own utterance, the personal experience has already been made a communal experience.

2.   See Kraus, *Psalms 1–59*, p. 355: 'The individual's experience of rescue is introduced in the congregation'. That is, in the framing of the psalm, the matter was never individual, it has always been communal. Here is an example of the way in which our conventional uses of genre have misread the text.

the extent to which Gunkel's genre reads what is there in the psalm, and the extent to which the stress on genre forces a reading that was not required either in the pre-exilic, cultic setting or in a later setting. The direction of my thinking then is that focus on the specific psalm may need to override genre analysis which is inevitably tempted to reductionism. The larger issue which Mays poses for me is whether we have confused early cultic religion in Israel and the tyranny of scholarly categories. Does a later use in fact break with early use, or does it simply resist our imposed categories? Our imposed categories may seduce us into slotting psalms in ways that are too rigid and simplistic.

3. On the contrast of ritual and instruction, I find the distinction difficult, for all ritual instructs and all serious communal instruction is in some sense construction as well as instruction. I do not fully understand how 'performance in the cult' and 'performance of the hymn' are to be related to each other. I wonder if this is a distinction drawn from the larger contrast of 'Israelite' and 'Jewish', on which I have commented earlier. I wonder then if the distinctions drawn by Mays do not reflect the imposition of categories from scholarship which would in fact not have been operative in the use of the Psalms. The either/or of cult/instruction may indeed be a false contrast derived from genre analysis and our dominant hypothesis of Israelite religion, that is, not derived from the Psalms themselves.

4. The observations Mays makes about the phenomena of combining, consolidating and comprehending genre, topics and motifs are surely correct. What is not clear to me is how much this matter of combining and consolidating is intrinsic to the Psalms themselves, and how much Mays's discernment is in fact an escape from long-established interpretive categories of scholars. Thus it is fair to ask about the combining of the 'divine work of creation and providence with the works of salvation history' in Psalms 136 and 145, how were they separated? Is such a separation the work of the old textual tradition, or is it rather the outcome of scholarly categories? And so with *ḥesed* and wisdom in Psalms 103–104. I do not know how one could determine that in the Psalms themselves and in Israel's religion itself, matters were originally separated, and to what extent such distinctions are made because of our modern propensity to classify and categorize. Or more broadly, is Mays noticing a dynamic process in the text of combining, consolidating and apprehending, or is he rather leading us out of the tyranny of analytical categories? Either way, his suggestion is an important gain,

but it is useful to think again about the nature of that gain.

5. Mays has suggested a fruitful line of intertextual work that should be pursued. I do not know how this particular enterprise, however, relates to the 'process' or 'context' of the Psalms under discussion. It may be enough to say that these poems—cultic or instructive—live in the world of Israel's memories and Israel's rhetoric. They will therefore inevitably be related to all of those resources and references to which Mays alludes. This is exactly what we should expect. While I do not see this as being closely related to our general topic, such allusions and connections are what we would expect in this on-going act of re-symbolization. In this point, Mays apparently takes up issues of intertextuality.

Mays has done exceedingly careful work on details and is able to identify remarkable linkages or coincidences. Presumably our work has not gone far enough or long enough to have any larger overview. The question of context is in the end, I believe, the invitation to try to the literature whole, and to interpret each of the parts in terms of the whole.

V

I wish to make one general comment and then to report on one specific piece of the Psalter (Psalm 73) which I have studied in greater detail. My general comment is with reference to Garrett Green's important book, *Imagining God*.[1] Green is informed by Thomas Kuhn's theory of paradigm and by Michael Polyani's notion of 'tacit knowledge'.[2] Green considers religious imagination as an act whereby one can see things whole, that is, according to a specific focus or lens, and thereby see things differently. Based in that religious phenomenology, Green then suggests that Christian imagination is the act of seeing matters whole according to an evangelical paradigm. Moreover, he proposes that the canon is the articulation of Christian paradigmatic imagination.[3]

---

1. G. Green, *Imagining God: Theology and the Religious Imagination* (San Francisco: Harper & Row, 1989). For a somewhat different approach to the same issues, see D.J. Bryant, *Faith and the Play of Imagination* (Macon, GA: Mercer University Press, 1989).

2. The influence of Kuhn in Green's book is crucial and visible. Green mentions Polyani only once (p. 107). It is nonetheless evident that the general approach of Polyani is operative, if not a direct influence upon Green.

3. Green, *Imagining God*, p. 116 and *passim*.

I refer to the general argument of Green because I want to see if his theoretical notion may provide a way to see the Psalter whole, and then to see if that canonical, paradigmatic whole will permit us to discern life through faith differently. That is, I suggest that while Mays's notion of process, movement and development in the book of Psalms is important, that notion in the end is in the service of his accent on context—the 'fabric of relations' between the various psalms.

I want now with impetus from Green's model to suggest six elements in seeing the Psalter whole.

1. It is recognized (and shrewdly handled by Mays) that Psalm 1 is intentionally and powerfully placed at the outset of the Psalter in order to provide a clue for the reading of the whole.[1] More succinctly, faith begins in obedience which is confident of God's faithful response.[2]

2. It is equally clear that Psalm 150 (or with Wilson, Psalms 145–150) is placed at the conclusion of the Psalter with intention.[3] Faith ends in praise, praise which is an act of utter, glad abandonment which depends upon no 'reason' and seeks no pay-out. Clearly the praise of Psalm 150 has moved dramatically beyond the obedience of Psalm 1 in terms of abandonment and trust.[4]

3. The canonical shape of the Psalter has as its problem movement

---

1. J.L. Mays, 'The Place of the Torah-Psalms in the Psalter', *JBL* 106 (1987), pp. 10-12. See also P.D. Miller, Jr, *Interpreting the Psalms* (Philadelphia: Fortress Press, 1986), pp. 82-86, and B.S. Childs, *Introduction to the Old Testament as Scripture* (Philadelphia: Fortress Press, 1979), pp. 513-14.

2. I am aware of the theological problems for conventional Christianity with the affirmation that faith begins in obedience. The canonical arrangement of the Psalter may require us to rethink our conventional notions of 'grace-law' which perhaps belong to particular historical crises. See the eloquent statement of A. Heschel, *Who is Man?* (Stanford: Stanford University Press, 1965), pp. 97-98. Notice also the poignant assertion of John Calvin, *Institutes of the Christian Religion* (ed. J.T. McNeill; The Library of Christian Classics, XX; Philadelphia: Westminster Press, 1960), p. 72, 'But not only faith, perfect and in every way complete, but all right knowledge of God is born of obedience'.

3. G.H. Wilson (*The Editing of the Hebrew Psalter* [SBLDS, 76; Chico, CA: Scholars Press, 1985], pp. 193-94) suggests that all of Psalms 145–150 serve as an intentional conclusion to the Psalter. While that may be, Psalm 150 is peculiar in its uncompromising and undistracted summons to praise.

4. In *Israel's Praise*, I have sought to understand Psalm 150 both critically and canonically. Critically, I have suggested that the psalm functions without reason and is readily available for ideology (pp. 92-93). Canonically, I have affirmed the positive function of Psalm 150, if not used 'too soon' (p. 155).

from Psalm 1 to Psalm 150, from a beginning in obedience to an ending in praise. I submit that this move is made as difficult as can be by the affirmation of Psalm 1, which is utterly confident about the claims of torah piety. The move is difficult because Psalm 1 guarantees that the problem of theodicy will emerge, for in fact God is clearly not one who causes the righteous to flourish and the wicked to disappear. If we do not reflect much, we can imagine a direct move from obedience to praise. The lived experience of Israel, however, will not permit such an easy, unreflective, direct move. The Psalter itself knows better. The material between beginning and end is the stuff of Israel's lived faith, the stuff whereby Israel processes the confident theodicy of Psalm 1 and the glad outcome of Psalm 150. Along the way, the move from the one to the other is troubled and complex, and often disordered.

4. Mays has observed that 'the crucial psalms for our purpose are those whose redaction or composition reflect the process of movement through stages of cultic history toward the formation of the book'. An example of this move must surely be Psalm 72. That psalm, in any conventional cultic hypothesis, functions in the royal cult. It is now placed, however, to close the second book of the Psalter which culminates in a doxology (v. 20). Moreover, the superscription, 'A Psalm of Solomon', further situates the psalm.[1] In my attempt to understand Mays's utilization of superscriptions,[2] I take this psalm to be a celebration of Solomonic well-being. When an appeal to historical Solomon is made, we know two things. First, Solomon's era was enormously blessed and prosperous. The psalm alludes to his prosperity:

> May he be like rain that falls on the mown grass,
>   like showers that water the earth!
> In his days may righteousness flourish,
>   and peace abound, till the moon be no more!
> May he have dominion from sea to sea...
> May all kings fall down before him,
>   all nations serve him (vv. 6-8, 11; RSV).

---

1.   The only other psalm with a Solomonic superscription is Psalm 127. That superscription seems to take the psalm with reference to temple building. I know of no scholarly comment on Psalm 127 concerning its canonical placement or function.

2.   B.S. Childs has contributed greatly to our understanding of the canonical function of the superscriptions and has formed some of the questions which we now must address. See Childs, *Introduction to the Old Testament as Scripture*, pp. 520-22, and 'Psalm Titles and Midrashic Exegesis', *JSS* 16 (1971), pp. 137-50.

The memory of Solomon's regime is cast in bold lyric.

The second thing we know is that Solomon's era ended in abrupt, hostile, and terrible misery and failure (1 Kings 11–12). That of course lies outside his celebrative psalm. Psalm 72 bespeaks the remembered blessing of the effective Solomon. It stops short of the failure of Solomon which was equally well known in Israel.

Wilson stresses that Psalm 72 is crucial for the Psalter and observes that Ps. 72.20 is a peculiar editorial element:

> Despite the existence of so many superscriptions (and one postscription) of obvious secondary origin (i.e., they do not form an integral part of the compositions they accompany, but evidence various secondary concerns), only *one* of these explicit statements can be said to exercise any organizational function. The exceptional case is the postscription preserved in Psalm 72:20: 'Finished are the prayers of David son of Jesse'. This comment makes it clear that a collection of compositions... attributed to a single author... has come to its conclusion... No other *explicit* indicators of segmentation can be isolated in MT 150.[1]

Thus Ps. 72.20 is an editorial marking that indicates an important turn in the collection. With this psalm for Solomon then, we have come to a fault in the Psalter marked by the concluding doxology. Given reasoning not unlike that of Mays concerning historical allusions, Psalm 72 ends by setting us in the midst of failure, revolutionary disruption, and exile.

The end of the Psalm, and the end of this collection, re-symbolize the end of Solomonic well-being, which in the canonical rendering, brings Israel to exile.[2]

5. I suggest that after Psalm 72 and its closure concerning Solomon, Psalm 73 is pivotally placed to see where faith can begin again, after the end of Solomon, after the end of royal effectiveness, after the monarchy and into exile. Ps. 73.1 of course has a well-known textual

---

1. Wilson, *Editing*, p. 139.
2. To take Solomon into the problem of the exile requires that Solomon should be taken canonically and not historically. That move from historical Solomon to canonical Solomon is accomplished in the Deuteronomic history, whereby the Solomonic materials in 1 Kings 3–11 are linked to the end of the monarchy. G.C. Macholz long ago (in personal communication) suggested to me that the oracle of Ahijah in 1 Kgs 11.31-32 was the beginning of the Deuteronomic program whereby land loss led eventually to exile. That understanding of Solomon vis-à-vis exile seems appropriate for Psalm interpretation in light of the centrality of 'torah-piety'.

problem; God is good either to 'Israel' or to the 'upright'.[1] With either reading, Ps. 73.1 sounds like an echo of Psalm 1. Thus the second half of the Psalter, after the end of Solomon, begins as does the first half, with an affirmation of God's faithfulness to the obedient. Psalm 73, however, departs drastically from Psalm 1 in its extended argument. The speaker is nearly reduced to unfaith (vv. 2-14), that is, away from the confident theodicy of Psalm 1. Only later does the speaker arrive back at a stronger, more confident faith in Yahweh's justice (vv. 17-26). It is probably important that the genre of Psalm 73 is problematic.[2] The uncertainty of genre perhaps bespeaks the uncertainty about Israel's faith after the collapse and end of the world of Psalm 72. In the face of such a collapse, the question of faith is how shall we speak, which implies not only what shall we say, but what genre is adequate?

I suggest that the turmoil reflected in Psalm 73 provides access to the more pervasive turmoil of faith reflected in the Psalter, expressed in the dialectic of hymns of faith and laments of protest. Thus the turmoil of the Psalter explicates the turmoil of displaced faith in exile. I suggest that Psalm 73 is a pivotal and probably distinctive point in the move from Psalm 1 to Psalm 150.

6. I will not go further with this line of questioning, except to make a large generalization about the sequence of Psalms 1, 72–73, 150. I suggest that canonical context requires a playful posture which at the same time insists on the claims of Psalm 1, and yet exposes Psalm 1 as false to experience. This latter exposé is voiced in laments and complaints. In order to move beyond the crises and break (of Psalm 72–73) to Psalm 150, however, a move of rhetoric and faith is required beyond protest toward profound trust in the God who keeps faith (though not as simply as in Psalm 1), and who therefore will be praised. That profound trust is voiced in praise and thanks. Thus the two genres of lament and complaint, and praise and thanks are essential

---

1. See E. Würthwein, 'Erwägungen zu Psalm 73', *Wort und Existenz* (Göttingen: Vandenhoeck & Ruprecht, 1970), pp. 161-78.

2. On the problematic character of Psalm 73, see J.F. Ross, 'Psalm 73', in J.G. Gammie, *et al.* (eds.), *Israelite Wisdom* (Missoula, MT: Scholars Press, 1978), pp. 161-75; J.L. Crenshaw, *A Whirlpool of Torment* (Philadelphia: Fortress Press, 1984), pp. 93-109; and J.C. McCann, 'Psalm 73: A Microcosm of Old Testament Theology', in K. Hoglund, *et al.* (eds.), *The Listening Heart* (JSOTSup, 58; Sheffield: JSOT Press, 1987), pp. 247-57.

voices in the move from Psalm 1 through Psalms 72–73 to Psalm 150. Except for attention to Psalms 72 and 73, I have moved in large strokes. I believe that if, as Green suggests, imagination is to see things whole, and canon is paradigmatic imagination, then we must look for clues concerning the whole. In terms of the function of the whole, we are permitted to see the Psalms as a dramatic struggle from obedience (Psalm 1) through dismay (Psalm 73 after 72) to praise (Psalm 150). If we are to say with Mays that we deal with a performance of a psalm rather than 'performance in the cult', this normative performance articulates and embraces faith across the break of the failure after Solomon, across the break after the extravagance of Psalm 72 and across the break of the exile. Thus we are prepared to see the Psalter as a dramatic whole, as a canonical, paradigmatic act of imagination that seeks to acknowledge the failure of a too simple theodic settlement (Psalm 1), but also to struggle with the theodic crisis voiced in the complaints as experienced and voiced in Judaism. It is then no wonder that the exilic, postexilic community appropriated old poems and hymns and liturgies in order to voice both its faith and its unfaith. Such an act of appropriation continues through the exile to be an act of daring, even a subversive act of symbolization, even if not done in a temple. That daring subversive act of symbolization happens in some public matrix which we may or may not call cult.

It remains for me to express my thanks to Professor Mays and my astonishment at the new problems he has unleashed. He has thought longer and better about these issues than anyone I know. It may be that I have seemed to disagree and challenge, but that is only because I had to write a response. It is his work which has provided the impetus for my thinking. It may be that my argument is too theological or thematic for his sober attention to editorial detail. I risk that, however, because as he has suggested, the issue concerns not anyone's proposal, even his, but our common attempt to understand a newly shaped problem. I will of course continue to work with the enormously rich suggestions he has offered us.[1]

---

1. For an elaboration of this attempt to understand the Psalter as a whole, see my essay 'Bounded by Obedience and Praise: The Psalms as Canon', *JSOT* 50 (1991), pp. 63-92.

UNDERSTANDING THE PURPOSEFUL ARRANGEMENT OF PSALMS IN THE PSALTER: PITFALLS AND PROMISE

Gerald H. Wilson

In the last decade renewed interest in the unity of the Psalter has uncovered evidence of the purposeful, editorial arrangement of the psalms.[1] The results of this process can be seen in the well known five-book structure of the Psalter as well as other evidence of theological and literary shaping of the materials.[2]

What remains unclear is just how far this editorial process of ordering observed in the larger structures of the Psalter extends to the consecutive arrangement of the individual psalms themselves. As a result of my own work, I am convinced that the final two books of the Psalter (Psalms 90–150) have been subjected to a thoroughgoing process of ordering following principles of arrangement quite distinct from those observed in the first three books (Psalms 2–89). This suggests to me the possibility of two separate periods of editorial activity behind these segments.[3] I remain uncertain just how the previous existence of earlier collections of psalms may have inhibited the freedom of arrangement of individual psalms in the first three books. In the last two books, where evidence of earlier collection is greatly reduced, arrangement would presumably have proceeded with less constraint. What is needed at this stage is a systematic investigation of the five books (including their subsections) to determine whether and to what extent evidence of purposeful arrangement of the individual compositions exists.

Some investigation has already been done focusing on various earlier

1. G.H. Wilson, *The Editing of the Hebrew Psalter* (SBLDS, 76; Chico, CA: Scholars Press, 1985).
2. G.H. Wilson, 'Evidence of Editorial Divisions in the Hebrew Psalter', *VT* 34 (1984), pp. 337-52.
3. Wilson, 'Evidence of Editorial Divisions'.

collections within the Psalter, but these have largely been concerned with analysis of form, theological content and social matrix of the collection, and less with arrangement.[1] Few have considered the relation of groups of psalms to the books in which they reside, or to the final form of the Psalter itself. However, some of these studies do provide information that proves valuable for those concerned with the larger question (especially linguistic and thematic links between consecutive and otherwise related psalms).

Other investigators have gone further and have attempted to demonstrate that the whole Psalter (not just Psalms 90–150) is the product of a systematic, purposeful and theologically motivated arrangement of individual psalms. To mount a successful and convincing demonstration of such a purposeful arrangement is far from easy, however. For one reason, the psalms have too long been read as isolated, individual compositions to be readily absorbed into an overarching theological framework that subordinates the single psalms to the ends of the whole. Another, perhaps more significant difficulty is that very few unambiguous signposts have been erected in this foreign territory, and the wary traveler must constantly guard against going astray by importing meaning to those few that can be found.

Despite the difficulty and ambiguity that attaches to this endeavor, I am convinced that such an investigation is possible, valuable, and, if pursued with appropriate caution, can be as fruitful as the past century of Psalms research. In what follows, I will comment from experience and observation on some pitfalls to be avoided and some promising pathways that may offer hope to those who choose to enter this brave new world.

John Walton, 'Psalms: A Cantata about the Davidic Covenant'

John Walton has recently suggested that the arrangement of the psalms in the Psalter could be explained as a 'cantata about the Davidic covenant'.[2] While I appreciate a number of individual insights that his

---

1. M.D. Goulder, *The Psalms of the Sons of Korah* (JSOTSup, 20; Sheffield: JSOT Press, 1982); C.C. Keet, *A Study of the Psalms of Ascent* (London: Mitre, 1969); H.P. Nasuti, *Tradition History and the Psalms of Asaph* (SBLDS, 88; Atlanta: Scholars Press, 1988); J.D.W. Watts, 'YHWH-Mālak Psalms', *TZ* 21 (1965), pp. 341-48.
2. J.H. Walton, 'Psalms: A Cantata About the Davidic Covenant', *JETS* 34.1

study presents, I question the starting point of his thesis, since it represents, in my opinion, one of the first and major pitfalls that must be avoided. At the outset of his investigation, Walton frames a 'working hypothesis' that provides 'a logical rationale for the ordering of the Psalms'. This hypothesis (that the Psalter is a Davidic cantata) is suggested, in Walton's view, by two elements of editorial structure emphasized in my own work—the function of Psalms 1 and 2 as introductions (to the Psalter and Book I respectively) and the theological progression of royal psalms placed at the 'seams' of the first three books (2, 41, 72, 89).[1]

Now, working hypotheses are a valid and useful means of research in the sciences where they can be tested repeatedly through experimentation in a controlled environment. They are, however, much more problematic in literary analysis where they can have the unfortunate effect of providing self-fulfilling prophecies. Especially in such a thematically diverse literature as the Psalms, a hypothesis set out beforehand can allow the researcher to see what supports the thesis and ignore what does not. I fear this to be the case in much of Walton's analysis. The thematic connections and linkages he suggests are tenuous at best and, while occasionally apt, are not ultimately convincing.

The strong influence of his hypothesis on the interpretation of psalms is further complicated by the fact that Walton moves from the warranted assumption that few (if any) of the psalms were composed specifically for the positions they now occupy to the unwarranted assumption that the editorial choice of a psalm for a particular position could be based on relatively trivial characteristics or phrases within the psalm and not its major themes. I can agree with Walton's first assumption without being impressed by the second. It is clear that the 150 psalms were not *composed* to function specifically in their present literary context. Certainly they were *selected* for that purpose from the vast wealth of hymnic compositions (now lost to us) that were originally developed for and employed chiefly in the ongoing

(1991), pp. 21-31.

1. See Walton, 'Psalms: A Cantata', pp. 23-24. As I have noted elsewhere ('The Use of Royal Psalms at the "Seams" of the Hebrew Psalter', *JSOT* 35 [1986], pp. 85-94), Psalm 41 is not generally recognized as a 'royal' psalm. The lack of such a psalm at this particular 'seam' may be explained by the earlier combination of Books I and II (2–72) into a unified collection as the postscript in 72.20 suggests.

worship of Israel. It is far from clear to me, however, that editors concerned to develop and communicate a theological message through the arrangement of the psalms would have selected compositions for relatively minor, even frivolous elements as Walton suggests.[1] This would have interrupted any continuity of thematic development and would ultimately have robbed the whole editorial process of its theological power! I can understand Walton's suggestion here only in that it allows him even more flexibility in the choice of elements that correspond to his predetermined hypothesis. It is no longer necessary for him to show how a *psalm* fits into the cantata schema, only some relatively minor element of a psalm. The possibilities for manipulation and circular reasoning (while not necessarily intentional) are drastically increased.

M.D. Goulder, 'The Fourth Book of the Psalter'

Similar tendencies and difficulties can be observed in the earlier article by M.D. Goulder concerning the arrangement of psalms in the fourth book (Psalms 90–106).[2] Goulder accepts the fact of the fivefold division of the Psalter and moves directly to the consideration of the fourth book as a unified collection. Like Walton he suggests what he considers an obvious working hypothesis that the fourth book was collected for liturgical purposes 'since the origin of many psalms is now agreed to be liturgical'.[3] He even goes so far as to suggest the specific liturgical setting for these psalms as the 'Autumn Festival'.[4] He bases this decision on the presence in these psalms of 'no less than nine different themes...which Mowinckel argued to be those of the Autumn Festival'.[5] What Goulder fails to note is that it is precisely on the basis of these psalms that Mowinckel developed his theory of the Autumn Festival and its thematic content. Could there be any doubt that these psalms would demonstrate the requisite themes? This is

---

1. A good example is Walton's explanation that Psalm 71 was placed at the point in the 'cantata' representing the end of David's reign because it contains a reference to 'old age'; see 'Psalms: A Cantata', pp. 24, 26.

2. M.D. Goulder, 'The Fourth Book of the Psalter', *JTS* 26 (1975), pp. 269-89.

3. Goulder, 'The Fourth Book of the Psalter', p. 269.

4. Goulder, 'The Fourth Book of the Psalter', p. 269.

5. Goulder, 'The Fourth Book of the Psalter', p. 269.

another clear example of the kind of circular reasoning that can accompany a working hypothesis faultily formulated to assume what it should in fact convincingly demonstrate.

Here we confront the questionable circumstance of a hypothetical festival serving as the interpretive filter through which the arrangement of the psalms is to be investigated. But, since Mowinckel's Autumn Festival is itself a hypothesis disputed by many, it remains in need of convincing proof before it can be employed as an established datum to confirm additional hypotheses. Otherwise we will be once again in the position of offering a self-fulfilling prophecy that can selectively interpret the data offered in these psalms. Just such a distortion is introduced, in my opinion, by Goulder's treatment of this festival liturgy as psalms presented alternately at evening and at morning.

Goulder arrives at this conclusion after a brief thematic analysis of Psalms 90–106 in which he notes an alternating pattern between the YHWH-*mālak* psalms (93, 97, 99) and those that emphasize singing a 'new song' (96, 98). While Goulder's minimal comments on the thematic links connecting this group of hymns are helpful, his subsequent step is more questionable. Noting that the festival is eight days in length and there are 17 psalms in this section, he suggests that the alternation 'might be explained if the psalms were in use at an alternating pattern of worship, such as morning and evening prayer'.[1]

Goulder then makes a brief investigation of the psalms and finds support for his conclusion that even-numbered psalms were evening psalms while odd-numbered psalms were recited in the morning. Such a conclusion is problematic since my own analysis of these 17 psalms indicates that six psalms (93, 98, 100, 103, 105, 106) make no clear temporal references; two psalms (91, 94) provide evidence that clearly contradicts the temporal reference Goulder demands; five psalms (92, 95, 96, 99, 104) are practically balanced in their temporal references; and only four psalms (90, 97, 101, 102) can be construed to support this alternating schema—some very questionably. Again the *assumption* of an alternating pattern makes it possible for the reader to interpret data to conform to the expectations of the hypothesis rather than to challenge and correct it or to develop a thesis from the demands of the data.

---

1.   Goulder, 'The Fourth Book of the Psalter', pp. 270-72.

Anton Arens, 'The Psalms in the Synagogue Lectionary Cycle'

One final example of the danger of allowing a working hypothesis to control the interpretation of data is found in the attempt of Anton Arens to explain the arrangement of the whole Psalter collection on the basis of the triennial synagogue lectionary system.[1] Noting the rabbinic connection of the five books of the Psalter with the five books of the Torah, Arens suggests that the arrangement of the psalms grows out of their use in the synagogue as accompaniment to the weekly reading of the Torah and Prophets. He then seeks to relate the individual psalms to the supposed Torah reading they accompanied.

As I have shown in more detail elsewhere,[2] Arens's construction runs into difficulty on several fronts. First, there is no general agreement on the number and extent of the Torah pericopes to which the 150 psalms must be related. Secondly, Arens's system requires the relocation of the end of the fourth book from Psalm 106 to Psalm 118—a move for which there is no evidence and which runs contrary to the presence of the doxology in 106.48. Thirdly, when Arens (and others) attempt to demonstrate thematic linkage between psalms and their supposed Torah passage, the connections suggested are consistently strained and ultimately unconvincing.[3] Surely, given the wealth of psalmic materials available during the exilic and postexilic periods, editors concerned to provide the Torah readings with psalmic support could have found more appropriate selections. The tenuous nature of those links adduced suggests they are secondary attempts to discover relationships where no real connection exists. This further illustrates the problem of allowing a working hypothesis to influence how one interprets the text.

Summary

My criticism thus far is directed to two major pitfalls that must be avoided if clear progress is to be made in analyzing the significance of the arrangement of the Psalms.

---

1.   A. Arens, *Die Psalmen im Gottesdienst des Alten Bundes* (Trier: Paulinus, 1968).

2.   Wilson, *Editing*, pp. 199-203.

3.   See the comments of H. J. Kraus, *Psalms 1–59* (trans. H.C. Oswald; Minneapolis: Augsburg-Fortress, 1988), pp. 20-21.

First, too many treatments of arrangement begin by setting forth an hypothesis to guide the investigation. Such working hypotheses, as we have seen, often distort the interpreter's vision and prevent the true nature of the material from coming into focus. In my opinion, the only valid and cautious hypothesis with which to begin is that the present arrangement is the result of purposeful editorial activity, and that its purpose can be discerned by careful and exhaustive analysis of the linguistic and thematic relationships between individual psalms and groups of psalms.

My second criticism is related to the first and is that too often the necessary in-depth analysis has not been done. The articulation of a hypothesis that *can* be supported is taken as confirmation of the truth of that hypothesis. A few, tenuous examples of agreement are considered sufficient proof. Where detailed analyses of the psalms have been done (even by those whose hypotheses I might resist) abundant insights have been gained and our understanding refined even though the hypothesis ultimately fails to convince.

My own preference is to work without a hypothesis (other than that cautious one mentioned above) and to allow any sense of the structure that develops to derive from an intensive and thorough analysis of the psalms in question in terms of their linguistic, thematic, literary and theological links and relationships. The good news is that some recent research into the arrangement of the psalms is proceeding cautiously and thoroughly and is basing its conclusions on data derived from this in-depth study of the psalms themselves.

J. Clinton McCann, 'Books I–III and the Editorial Purpose of the Hebrew Psalter'

One such study by Clint McCann responds to earlier insights regarding the placement of royal psalms at the 'seams' of the first three books of the Psalter and the suggestion that the fourth and fifth books serve as a theological reply to the problem of the failed Davidic covenant presented in the first three books.[1] McCann seeks to show that the attempt to deal with the negative experience of the exile has also left its imprint on the first three books. He focuses initially on the seam psalms that open the first three books (rather than the closing seam

---

1.   See Wilson, 'The Use of Royal Psalms'.

psalms previously studied). He is able to show by careful linguistic analysis close linkages between Psalms 73–74 and 42, 43 and 44 suggesting more than accidental juxtaposition at work here.

McCann's further analysis in Book III (Psalms 73–89) uncovers an alternating pattern of lament–hope throughout this book. He suggests that the pattern is intended to help the suffering exilic community 'to reach a reorientation based upon the rejection of the Davidic/Zion theology that had formerly been Judah's primary grounds of hope. The canonical juxtaposition of the traditional Davidic/Zion theology with community psalms of lament serves to signal the rejection of this basis of hope.'[1] While these results augment my own work and conclusions, McCann's results are based ultimately on his own careful analysis and will stand or fall on his ability to interpret the data of the text persuasively.

David M. Howard, 'The Structure of Psalms 93–100'

Another example of careful attention to the details of linguistic and literary analysis is the recent PhD dissertation of David M. Howard, Jr.[2] Howard's work sets out to describe 'the internal structure of a specific corpus within the Psalter: Psalms 93–100'.[3] Here, as all dissertations demand, Howard's attention to detail is commendable. In a chapter of some 100 pages, Howard presents a linguistic and thematic analysis of each individual psalm in this section. Then, in an additional 60 pages, he considers each psalm thus analyzed in its relation to each of the others. A final chapter then employs the results of this study to discuss the significance of the structure of this whole grouping.

His thematic and linguistic analysis leads Howard to conclude that Psalms 95 and 100 'form an inclusion around the Kingship group in 96–99'.[4] This decision is based on what Howard calls 'close lexical correspondences' and the 'almost identical structure and content of 95.6b-7c and 100.3b-c'.[5] The detailed study allows Howard to discern

---

1. See J.C. McCann, Jr, 'Books I–III and the Editorial Purpose of the Hebrew Psalter' in the present volume.
2. D.M. Howard, Jr, 'The Structure of Psalms 93–100' (PhD dissertation, University of Michigan, Ann Arbor, 1986).
3. Howard, 'The Structure of Psalms *93–100*', abstract.
4. Howard, 'The Structure of Psalms *93–100*', p. 207.
5. Howard, 'The Structure of Psalms *93–100*', p. 207.

a clear structure for this group of psalms that 'stands as the "center" of Book IV, both positionally and thematically'.[1]

While it is unfortunate that Howard limited his detailed study to Psalms 93–100 rather than extending his analysis to the whole of Book IV (Psalms 90–106), this oversight is mitigated somewhat by his discussion of the smaller collection's place within its larger literary context.[2] The lack of attention to the broader context accounts for Howard's failure to understand the function of the positioning of Psalm 94, with its clear connections to the earlier complex of Psalms 90–92, between the initial YHWH-*mālak* psalm (93) and the major collection of these psalms in 95–99. The broader perspective indicates that the transposition of the final psalm of the first group and the beginning psalm of the second group is an accepted editorial technique to bind two segments together into a new whole.[3]

Conclusions

As must be obvious by now, I am convinced that any progress in understanding the purposeful arrangement of the psalms in the Psalter must begin, as in these last two studies, with a detailed and careful analysis of the linguistic, literary and thematic linkages that can be discerned among the psalms. Analysis of the arrangement of psalms must proceed from (1) the recognition of clear indications of psalms groupings where discernible (by doxologies, author designations, genre indications, *hllwyh-hwdw* groupings)[4] to (2) the detailed and systematic investigation of linguistic and thematic connections between psalms within these groupings and their subgroups. Only at this point (3) can judicious speculation begin to be made regarding the purpose or effects of the arrangement of the whole Psalter. Finally, and perhaps never with complete certainty, will it be possible (4) to make

---

1.   Howard, 'The Structure of Psalms *93–100*', p. 217.

2.   Howard, 'The Structure of Psalms *93–100*', pp. 199-217.

3.   A similar, more complex binding arrangement can be observed at work in the interweaving of the Qorahite, Asaphite and Davidic collections in the second and third books (Psalms 42–89). See my discussion of this arrangement in 'Shaping the Psalter: A Consideration of Editorial Linkage in the Book of Psalms' in the present volume.

4.   For a discussion of the use of *hllwyh* and *hwdw* psalms to segment the last two books of the Psalter, see Wilson, 'Evidence of Editorial Divisions'.

suggestions as to the appropriate social/historical matrix that may illuminate the theological function and purpose revealed by the editorial arrangement.

We now stand on the borders of the promised land. Like Moses' spies, we need to take care to learn the lay of the land and to acquire an intimate knowledge of its inhabitants, lest we be misled by our own preconceived notions to see giants where there are none and lest we, because of our misconceptions, fail to take the land.

Editorial Activity in the Psalter: A State-of-the-Field Survey[*]

David M. Howard, Jr

Introduction

This essay is intended to survey the state of the field in the study of editorial processes in the formation of the Psalter, and is intended to highlight some common ground among the many scholars working in this area. It briefly surveys the mainstream approaches and then focuses on studies dealing with editorial activity in some way. The new interest in editorial activity clearly is related to the current trend in biblical studies toward unitary, literary and 'canonical' readings of the Bible. It is particularly a challenge in Psalms studies, however, due to the obviously independent and self-contained nature of the individual psalms. Despite this, many advances are being made and much can be said about the concerns of the Psalter's editors.

Mainstream Approaches to Psalms Study

Early interest in the Psalms in Christian circles was dominated for the most part by allegorical or messianic concerns, prior to the rise of modern critical scholarship.[1] With the rise of critical scholarship in the nineteenth century, interest shifted to the historical backgrounds of the

 * Original essay appeared in *WW* 9.3 (Summer 1989), pp. 274-85. Copyright 1989 Luther Northwestern Theological Seminary. Reprinted (with minor additions) with permission of *Word & World*.

 1. J.M. Neale and R.F. Littledale, *A Commentary on the Psalms: From Primitive and Medieval Writers* (4 vols.; London: Joseph Masters, 3rd edn, 1874–1879); B.K. Waltke, 'A Canonical Process Approach to the Psalms', in J.S. Feinberg and P.D. Feinberg (eds.), *Tradition and Testament* (Festschrift C.L. Feinberg; Chicago: Moody, 1981), pp. 3-5.

biblical materials, including radical reconstruction of the biblical text.[1] Modern Psalms study was radically reshaped by the well-known work of H. Gunkel.[2] Now the attention was focused on the forms (that is, genres) of individual psalms, and attention was paid to the *Sitz im Leben* that gave rise to each form. Since the psalms were not arranged according to genre, the work of Gunkel and all indebted to him since has ranged throughout the Psalter, collecting and discussing together the psalms of the various genres. At the same time, attention continued to be paid, in varying degrees, to matters of authorship and historical reconstruction (the search for the *Sitz im Leben*).

S.O.P. Mowinckel's work[3] followed Gunkel's in classifications, but cleared its own way in emphasizing especially the cultic background to almost all the psalms.[4] In addition, Mowinckel's great influence has been felt in his view that the major festival in Israel was the harvest and new-year festival, the centerpiece of which was the so-called 'Enthronement of YHWH' festival.[5]

Almost all work since these two has reflected their influence. The focus has been on forms and (cultic) *Sitz im Leben*, with little interest in the question of inter-psalm links.[6] The most that the majority of

1. Representative of this period and approach are the works of G.H.A.V. Ewald, *Commentary on the Psalms* (trans. E. Johnson; 2 vols.; London: Williams & Norgate, 1880); J.J.S. Perowne, *The Book of Psalms* (2 vols.; Andover: Warren F. Draper, 7th edn, 1890); T.K. Cheyne, *The Origins and Religious Contents of the Psalter in the Light of Old Testament Criticism and the History of Religions* (New York: Whittaker, 1891); *idem The Book of Psalms* (2 vols.; London: Kegan, Paul, Touch, 1904); J. Wellhausen, *The Book of Psalms* (Polychrome Bible; London: James Clark, 1898); C.A. Briggs and E.G. Briggs, *A Critical and Exegetical Commentary on the Book of Psalms* (2 vols.; International Critical Commentary; New York: Charles Scribner's Sons, 1906).

2. H. Gunkel, *Die Psalmen* (Göttinger Handkommentar zum Alten Testament; Göttingen: Vandenhoeck & Ruprecht, 4th edn, 1926); *Einleitung in Die Psalmen* (ed. J. Begrich; Göttingen: Vandenhoeck & Ruprecht, 2nd edn, 1933).

3. S.O.P. Mowinckel, *Psalmenstudien* (6 vols.; Kristiana: Jacob Dybwad, 1921–1924); *The Psalms in Israel's Worship* (trans. D.R. Ap-Thomas; 2 vols.; Nashville: Abingdon Press, 1962).

4. The few 'wisdom' psalms excepted; see *The Psalms in Israel's Worship*, II, pp. 104-25.

5. Mowinckel, *Psalmenstudien*. II. *Das Thronbesteigungfest Jawäs und der Ursprung der Eschatologie* (1921); *The Psalms in Israel's Worship*, I, pp. 106-92.

6. Typical are the following: H. Schmidt, *Die Psalmen* (HAT, 15; Tübingen: Mohr [Paul Siebeck], 1934); J. Calès, *Le livre des Psaumes* (2 vols.; Paris: Gabriel

commentators have done concerning the question of the organization of the Psalter (or of portions therein) is to note the division into five 'books' (Psalms 1–41, 42–72, 73–89, 90–106, 107–150), marked by doxologies, and to note some of the various collections or pseudo-collections within these 'books'. Examples of these are the *ma'ălôt* psalms (120–134), the Asaphic (73–83) and Korahite (42–49, 84–85, 87–88) collections, the Elohistic psalter (42–83), or the *maśkîl* groups (42–45, 52–55). For the most part, there has been no real interest in the internal structures of these collections, except the casual noting that they were somehow liturgical in nature. The more specific questions of organization and structure *within* these groupings have gone unaddressed in the main.

Studies Devoted to Inter-Psalm Relationships

a. *Pre-1970s*
The rabbis and early Christian commentators traditionally were more interested in questions of inter-psalm relationships than were later Christian scholars. Their works especially reflected attention to catch-word (or key-word) links between consecutive psalms ('concatenation').[1] Often, these links involved key words at the end

---

Beauchesne, 5th edn, 1936); W.O.E. Oesterley, *A Fresh Approach to the Psalms* (New York: Charles Scribner's Sons, 1937); *The Psalms: Translated with Text-Critical and Exegetical Notes* (London: SPCK, 1939); M. Buttenwieser, *The Psalms: Chronologically Treated with a New Translation* (Chicago: University of Chicago Press, 1938); E.A. Leslie, *The Psalms: Translated and Interpreted in the Light of Hebrew Life and Worship* (New York: Abingdon Press, 1949); F. Nötscher, *Die Psalmen* (Echter Bibel; Wurzburg: Echter, 1952); M.E.J. Kissane, *The Book of Psalms* (2 vols.; Dublin: Richview, 1954); A. Weiser, *The Psalms* (trans. H. Hartwell; OTL; Philadelphia: Westminster Press, 1962); L. Sabourin, *The Psalms: Their Origin and Meaning* (2 vols.; Staten Island, NY: Alba House, 1969); A.A. Anderson, *The Book of Psalms* (2 vols.; New Century Bible Commentary; Grand Rapids: Eerdmans, 1972); D. Kidner, *Psalms 1–150* (2 vols.; TOTC; Downers Grove, IL: IVP, 1973, 1975); H.-J. Kraus, *Psalmen* (2 vols.; BKAT, 15/1-2; Neukirchen: Neukirchener Verlag, 1978); P.C. Craigie, *Psalms 1–50* (WBC, 19; Waco, TX: Word Books, 1983). M.J. Dahood's work (*Psalms I–III* [AB 16-17A Garden City, NY: Doubleday, 1966–1970]) represented a major departure of approach in his attention to Ugaritic materials, but he likewise had brief sections on forms and showed no real interest in the questions of organization.
    1.   J.P. Brennan, 'Some Hidden Harmonies in the Fifth Book of the Psalms',

of one psalm and the beginning of the next.[1] Even after the rise of critical scholarship, we can see some limited interest in relationships between psalms and in the Psalter's structure. Already in the nineteenth century, Franz Delitzsch had paid considerable attention to the connections between consecutive psalms.[2] He saw links of thoughts or ideas between consecutive psalms, and saw these running topically throughout the Psalter.[3] He stated that,

> This phenomenon, that psalms with similar prominent thoughts, or even with only markedly similar passages, especially at the beginning and the end, are thus strung together, may be observed throughout the whole collection.[4]

He saw in the arrangement of the Davidic psalms throughout the Psalter the key to the unifying motif in the book, namely, a concern with the Davidic covenant and, ultimately, a messianic concern.

J.A. Alexander's work likewise was sensitive to links, and he devoted a major section of his introduction to the coherence within the Psalter.[5] He saw the messianic motif as the overall one, with the Davidic covenant given a prominent place.[6] He discussed several possible principles of arrangement, the most relevant one here being that juxtaposition of psalms was often due to 'resemblance or identity of subject or historical occasion, or in some remarkable coincidence of general form or of particular expressions'.[7] He admitted that in some cases the connections are easier to see than others, but stated that,

in R.F. McNamara (ed.), *Essays in Honor of Joseph P. Brennan* (Rochester, NY: St Bernard's Seminary, 1976), p. 126.

1. See U. Cassuto, 'The Sequence and Arrangement of the Biblical Sections', in *Biblical and Oriental Studies*, I (trans. I. Abrahams; Jerusalem: Magnes, 1973), pp. 1-6, for a brief, but wide-ranging essay on this principle, which he termed 'verbal association'.

2. That is the major thrust of Delitzsch's 1846 work (*Symbolae ad Psalmos illustrandos isagogicae* [Leipzig], referred to in his *Biblical Commentary on the Psalms* [trans. F. Bolton; 3 vols.; Grand Rapids: Eerdmans, 1881, repr. 1975], I, p. 17), and it is seen in the commentary as well.

3. Delitzsch, *Biblical Commentary*, I, pp. 15-23, and *passim* throughout the commentary proper.

4. Delitzsch, *Biblical Commentary*, I, p. 21.

5. J.A. Alexander, *The Psalms* (3 vols.; New York: Charles Scribner's Sons, 6th edn, 1865), pp. vii-xiv.

6. Alexander, *The Psalms*, pp. xiv-xv.

7. Alexander, *The Psalms*, pp. ix.

> Sometimes, particularly in the latter part of the collection, we may trace not only pairs but trilogies and even more extensive systems of connected psalms, each independent of the rest, and yet together forming beautiful and striking combinations, particularly when the nucleus or basis of the series is an ancient psalm, for instance one of David's, to which others have been added, in the way of variation or of imitation, at a later period, such as that of the Captivity.[1]

Alexander's commentary proper shows careful attention to details of possible connections between psalms, including key words, motifs and even grammatical constructions.

Since Delitzsch and Alexander, however, very few commentaries have reflected these concerns. That of A.F. Kirkpatrick[2] and two popular Jewish commentaries—those of A. Cohen[3] and S.R. Hirsch[4]—are the notable exceptions. The first two observed the key-word connections between psalms, but attempted no real analysis beyond that. Hirsch's comments were limited to telling the 'story' of the psalms in terms of Israel's exilic experiences.

Westermann's article on the formation of the Psalter also is a significant exception.[5] In this essay, he made seven distinctive observations, several of which anticipated the work of Childs and Wilson (see below). The most significant is that the collections of individual laments tend to group early in the Psalter, mainly in Books I and II, and that the great praise collections tend to group toward the end, mainly in Books IV and V.[6] Secondly, he noted the function of certain praise psalms in closing small collections of psalms (for example, Psalms 18–19, 33–34, 40, 65–66, 100, 117, 134). He also noted the function of royal psalms as part of the Psalter's framework.

1. Alexander, *The Psalms*, pp. ix-x.
2. A.F. Kirkpatrick, *The Book of Psalms* (Cambridge: Cambridge University Press, 1901).
3. A. Cohen, *The Psalms* (Soncino Books of the Bible; London: Soncino, 1945).
4. S.R. Hirsch, *The Psalms* (trans. G. Hirschler; 2 vols.; New York: Philip Feldheim, 1960, 1966).
5. C. Westermann, 'Zur Sammlung des Psalters', *Theologia Viatorum* 8 (1962), pp. 278-84, translated as 'The Formation of the Psalter', in *Praise and Lament in the Psalms* (trans. K.R. Crim and R.N. Soulen; Atlanta: John Knox, 1981), pp. 250-58.
6. In this way, the outline of the Psalter as a whole mirrors the outline of the lament itself—both end with movements toward praise.

b. *1970s and 1980s*

Recently there has emerged a more steady stream of works concerned with the links and overall motifs in the Psalter, though it is still a trickle in comparison with the volume of studies oriented in other directions. M.D. Goulder has studied this with reference to liturgical aspects of collections in the Psalter.[1] In discussing the tendencies to classify the psalms, with the attendant random study of many psalms, he stated that,

> The dazzled student soon suppresses as naive his instinct that it is proper to study [Psalm] 1 before [Psalm] 2, and that there is something curious in beginning a book on the Psalter with the 110th, or 89th psalm... The instinct that the order of the psalms may be important is not however naive, and is far from irrational... [I]t is entirely proper to begin the study of the Psalter with the expectation that it will be an ordered and not an assorted collection; or, at the very least, that it will contain elements that were rationally ordered.[2]

In a similar way, J.P. Brennan has stated the underlying presupposition typical of such efforts:

> A careful reading indicates that the Psalter has not developed in a haphazard and arbitrary way, but has been carefully woven together in such a manner that previously independent compositions, or smaller collections of such compositions, now comment upon or respond to one another. Hence, for a proper understanding of the Psalter it is not enough to study each of its 150 components in the historical context from which it originally sprang. They must all be studied in their relationship to each other, since all of them together convey more than they do if looked at separately.[3]

Brennan first studied Book V of the Psalter (Psalms 107–150), and he saw the governing principles of the final collection as literary, not liturgical,[4] and his work traced the key-word connections therein. Later,[5] he more directly stated that not only was there an internal coherence in the Psalter, but that there was a unifying motif, that of wisdom, capable of being traced throughout the Psalter, especially in linking consecutive psalms. That is to say, while the original *Sitz im*

---

1. M.D. Goulder, 'The Fourth Book of Psalter', *JTS* 26 (1975), pp. 269-89; *The Psalms of the Sons of Korah* (JSOTSup, 20; Sheffield: JSOT Press, 1982).
2. Goulder, *Psalms of the Sons of Korah*, p. 8.
3. Brennan, 'Hidden Harmonies', pp. 126-27.
4. Brennan, 'Hidden Harmonies', p. 128.
5. J.P. Brennan, 'Psalms 1–8: Some Hidden Harmonies', *BTB* 10 (1980), pp. 25-29.

Leben of individual psalms and even small collections in the Psalter was the cult, and the 'I' of many of the psalms was the Davidic king, the reader of the Psalter in its final form was to read it as a book, and not necessarily perform it or use it in a liturgy. Thus, the 'I' was now each individual reader. Brennan concluded that,

> Such a reading of the Psalter opens the way to an eschatological and messianic interpretation of many texts which had originally only a limited national and historic setting. The Psalter comes to be seen as a magnificent dramatic struggle between the two ways—that of Yahweh, his anointed king, and the company of the just, and that of the wicked, the sinners, the evil-doers.[1]

In reaching this conclusion, Brennan put much stock in the significance of the content and placement of Psalms 1 and 2. Psalm 1, a Torah psalm, clearly lays out the two ways, thus setting the stage for a reading of the entire book as reflective of the struggle between them. Psalm 2 is a royal psalm, and its placement makes clear that the memory of the Davidic king was to be kept alive even after the fall of the monarchy.

This attention to Psalms 1 and 2, and especially Psalm 1, as the heading for the Psalter, is not unique to Brennan. Most introductions and commentaries note this in passing, and note that while the Masoretic Text (MT) of the Psalter carries superscriptions for only 116 psalms, the Septuagint (LXX) carries superscriptions for all but Psalms 1 and 2, lending credence to this idea.

What is new with Brennan—and many others recently—is the emphasis on the confluence of placement and content of these two psalms (or at least Psalm 1) in having a determining effect upon reading of the rest of the Psalter.

In his *Introduction*, B.S. Childs likewise focused on the final form of the Psalter and saw eschatological reinterpretation as the governing motif for it.[2] He stated that,

> Although the royal psalms arose originally in a peculiar historical setting of ancient Israel which had received its form from a common mythopoetic milieu, they were treasured in the Psalter for a different reason, namely as a witness to the messianic hope which looked for the consummation of God's kingship through his Anointed One.[3]

1. Brennan, 'Psalms 1–8', p. 29.
2. B.S. Childs, *Introduction to the Old Testament as Scripture* (Philadelphia: Fortress Press, 1979), pp. 504-25.
3. Childs, *Introduction*, p. 517.

Childs saw—more clearly than Westermann had—the royal psalms as the backbone of the Psalter, noting that they were not grouped together, but rather were strategically scattered throughout the collection; and he also emphasized the placement of Psalm 2. This served to underline the kingship of God as a major theme throughout the entire collection.[1]

For Childs, the significance of Psalm 1's placement is in its being a Torah psalm; it functions as a preface to the book, signaling that everything that follows is, in effect, God's Torah, to be read, studied and meditated upon. In doing so, the faithful reader would reap the blessings promised in Psalm 1. The words of people to God had now become identified with God's word to God's people:

> Israel reflects on the psalms, not merely to find an illustration of how godly men prayed to God in the past, but to learn the 'way of righteousness' which comes from obeying the divine law and is now communicated through the prayers of Israel.[2]

G.T. Sheppard, a student of Childs, agrees with him that Psalms 1–2 form the 'Preface' to the Psalter.[3] After noting some of the specific lexical links between the sapiential Psalm 1 and the royal Psalm 2, he summarizes their general relationship:

> The profane nations and rulers in Ps. 2 are identified with those who walk the way of sinners and the wicked in Ps. 1. Opposite these, one finds the divine king depicted in the language of Nathan's oracle as one who, by contrastive implication, walks in the way of the righteous. Consequently, David is represented in Ps. 2 both as the author of the Psalms and also as one who qualifies under the injunction of Ps. 1 to interpret the Torah as a guide to righteousness.[4]

---

1.   Childs, *Introduction*, pp. 515-16. This idea has now been developed more fully by his student, G.H. Wilson, 'The Use of Royal Psalms at the "Seams" of the Hebrew Psalter', *JSOT* 35 (1986), pp. 85-94. The Kingdom of God as 'the organizing, unifying subject of the psalter' (p. 155) is discussed in connection with the prominence of David—as king, the agent of God's reign on earth—by J.L. Mays in 'The David of the Psalms', *Int* 40 (1986), pp. 143-55.

2.   Childs, *Introduction*, pp. 513-14.

3.   G.T. Sheppard, *Wisdom as a Hermeneutical Construct: A Study in the Sapientializing of the Old Testament* (BZAW, 151; Berlin: de Gruyter, 1980), pp. 136-44.

4.   Sheppard, *Wisdom as a Hermeneutical Construct*, p. 142.

He goes on to say that,

> By his association with Ps. 2, David, who is, in canonical terms, the chief
> architect of the Psalter, is fully in accord with the ideals of Ps. 1. The
> entire Psalter, therefore, is made to stand theologically in association with
> David as a source of guidance for the way of the righteous. In this
> fashion, the Psalter has gained, among its other functions, the use as a
> source for Wisdom reflection and a model of prayers based on such a
> pious interpretation of the Torah.[1]

J. Reindl, in a programmatic essay,[2] also argues along these lines
(although he ignores the implications of the dominant royal motifs in
the Psalter). He reviews some of the literature devoted to the question
of the organization of the canonical Psalter and finds it deficient—either
because it is skeptical about any organizing principle, or because it
sees the principle as being solely liturgical. He notes with approval
C. Barth's essay on concatenation, which argued that there was another
principle at work than just the liturgical.[3] He sees Psalm 1 as Brennan,
Childs and Sheppard do, as a sort of opening speech (*Prooemium*) for
the reader and 'pray-er' of the psalms, setting out the two ways.[4] The
'and in his Torah he meditates day and night' of Ps. 1.2b is literally
meant, and even the Psalter is part of God's Torah. He states that,

> The original *Sitz im Leben* [of each individual psalm] pales into insig-
> nificance (though it does not disappear) in the face of the new *Sitz im
> Leben* which the Psalter has received.[5]

Accordingly, Reindl does not see the final redactor(s) of the Psalter as
being a part of the temple singers, but rather as belonging to the
circles of scribes, ones following the piety of the Torah, who followed
the way of the wise in older times and who pursued the ideal picture
painted of Jesus Sirach (Sir. 39.1-11).[6]

---

1. Sheppard, *Wisdom as a Hermeneutical Construct*, p. 142.
2. J. Reindl, 'Weisheitliche Bearbeitung von Psalmen: Ein Beitrag zum
Verständnis der Sammlung des Psalter', in J.A. Emerton (ed.), *Congress Volume,
Vienna 1980* (VTSup, 32; Leiden: Brill, 1981), pp. 333-56.
3. See below, p. 66 n. 4.
4. Reindl, 'Weisheitliche Bearbeitung', pp. 338-39.
5. Reindl, 'Weisheitliche Bearbeitung', p. 340 (translation mine). He also cites
(p. 338, n. 15) his article 'Psalm 1 und der Sitz im Leben des Psalters'
(*Theologisches Jahrbuch* [Leipzig: St Benno, 1979], pp. 39-50), in which he
develops this further, but I have been unable to locate a copy of it.
6. Reindl, 'Weisheitliche Bearbeitung', pp. 340-41.

If this be the case, then one could expect the editor(s) of the Psalter to leave traces of their work. Besides the example of Psalm 1 and its placement, Reindl offers several other texts in support of his thesis. Each of these appears to have been a gloss, interrupting the texts, usually toward the ends of them. The three individual texts he treats are Pss. 50.16a; 146.8b, 9b; 104.35.[1] Each of these introduces a sudden shift in topic, and is concerned with a traditional wisdom motif. He then treats Psalms 90–92 as a group,[2] showing them to occur at a strategic location in the Psalter, namely, between the first half of the Psalter, where the organizing principle is fairly clear (Davidic Psalter, Elohistic Psalter, plus appendix), and the second, where the rationale is not so clear. Here, too, he sees a decided wisdom flavor.

Reindl lays out four possible consequences of his study.[3]

1. The 'wisdom editing' of the Psalter that he attempts to show should be capable of easy detection throughout the rest of the Psalter, the redactor's hand being seen in glosses or text expansions.

2. The question of the arrangement in the redactional context should not be neglected in exegesis of individual psalms, as he shows especially in the cases of Psalms 90–92.

3. For the Psalter in its revised, final form, a different *Sitz im Leben* from its earlier, liturgical one can be seen. Psalms study should not limit itself to study of only one (often hypothetical) early *Sitz im Leben*.

4. The psalms, originally the words of people to God, now became the words of God to people, suitable for study and meditation, by virtue of the 'canonical' outlook, searched for and found in them by the scribes responsible for the final editing. In the end, the idea of the Psalter as being *God's* word (and not humanity's) 'had as much significance for the reception [as canonical] of the already existing book in the developing canon as did its use in the cult'.[4]

The similarities between Reindl's thesis and those of Brennan, Childs and Sheppard should be clear. All four emphasize (1) a literary

1. Reindl, 'Weisheitliche Bearbeitung', pp. 344-50.
2. Reindl, 'Weisheitliche Bearbeitung', pp. 350-55.
3. Reindl, 'Weisheitliche Bearbeitung', pp. 355-56.
4. Reindl, 'Weisheitliche Bearbeitung', p. 356 (translation mine).

rationale as responsible for the final form of the Psalter, (2) that this rationale reflects a non-liturgical *Sitz im Leben*, (3) that an individualizing tendency can be seen in the use of the psalms and (4) that wisdom motifs play some part in the scheme.[1]

A recent—and the most comprehensive—treatment of the question of the structure of the Psalter is that of G.H. Wilson, a student of Childs, to whom he is indebted for much of the framework of ideas.[2] He lays the methodological foundations that the others do not have, in tracing other examples of collections of hymnic material from the ancient Near East —the Sumerian Temple Hymn Collection and Catalogues of Hymnic Incipits (chs. 2, 3) and the Qumran psalms manuscripts (chs. 4, 5). Each of these exhibits definite editorial techniques in the outlines of their final forms. He then turns to the canonical Hebrew Psalter and looks for evidence of editorial principles (chs. 6, 7). He finds two types of evidence, namely, explicit and tacit (that is, non-explicit). For Wilson, 'explicit' indicators are found in the psalm superscriptions or in the postscript to Books I–II at Ps. 72.20, while 'tacit' indicators are found in editorial arrangements, such as the grouping of psalms with doxologies at the ends of Books I–IV of the Psalter, or the grouping of the *hallelu-yah* psalms (104–106, 111–117, 135, 146–150) at the ends of certain Psalter segments.[3]

Like the others, Wilson gives prominence to the placement and contents of Psalms 1 and 2. The psalms in their final collection are meant to be read and meditated upon (Psalm 1). The Davidic king and the Davidic covenant are prominent throughout (Psalm 2). This latter concern is seen not only by the predominance of David in the superscriptions, but also in the appearance of royal psalms at the 'seams' of the first three books (Psalms 2, 72, 89).[4]

Book IV (Psalms 90–106) stands at the editorial 'center' of the final Psalter:

---

1.   See also Westermann, 'The Formation of the Psalter', where he made most of the same points.

2.   G.H. Wilson, *The Editing of the Hebrew Psalter* (SBLDS, 76; Chico, CA: Scholars Press, 1985).

3.   Wilson, *Editing*, pp. 9-10, 182-97.

4.   Wilson, *Editing*, pp. 207-14; 'Royal Psalms'. (The end of the first Davidic collection at Psalm 41 accounts for the remaining seam.)

As such this grouping stands as the 'answer' to the problem posed in Ps. 89 as to the apparent failure of the Davidic covenant with which Books One–Three are primarily concerned. Briefly summarized the answer given is: (1) YHWH is king; (2) He has been our 'refuge' in the past, long before the monarchy existed (i.e., in the Mosaic period); (3) He will continue to be our refuge now that the monarchy is gone; (4) Blessed are they that trust in him![1]

Book V is rather heterogeneous, but an attitude of dependence and trust on YHWH alone can be seen as the model encouraged there (see especially Ps. 107.12-13, 19, 28, at the head of Book V). David is seen as modeling this attitude in Psalms 108–110 and 138–145, an attitude which finds expression in obedience to YHWH's Torah, expressed in the massive and centrally located Psalm 119. The psalms of ascents (Psalms 120–134) express repeated reliance on YHWH alone. The section concludes with the great doxologies of Psalms 146–150, including the theme of YHWH's kingship in Psalms 146–147 which has dominated Book IV and which stands in contrast to the fragile picture of human kingship in Psalms 2–89. YHWH alone is the eternal king, and YHWH alone is worthy of trust in the end.[2]

There are other scholars working along these lines (of connections between adjacent psalms and within larger collections) who are not as self-consciously interested in editorial processes and literary activity as those scholars noted above, but whose results are similar. These include K. Seybold, P. Auffret, T. Collins and M.D. Goulder.

Seybold's is the most sophisticated work to date on the psalms of ascents, in terms of accounting for their origin and development.[3] He analyzed these as originally rural pilgrimage psalms, which were redacted by editors with a Zion/Temple ideology to form a collection fit for the pilgrimage to Jerusalem. He noted that the repetitions of Zion/Temple motifs tend to occur at the end or beginning of the poems, or else at spots where they repeat (clumsily, in his view) catch-words or catch-lines in the original 'rural' poems. An advantage of this approach is that it sees a coherence between these texts that undoubtedly reflects some of the ancient situation. The obvious danger is the

---

1. Wilson, *Editing*, p. 215.
2. Wilson, *Editing*, pp. 220-28.
3. K. Seybold, *Die Wallfahrtpsalmen: Studien zur Enstehungsgeschichte von Psalmen 120–134* (Biblische-Theologische Studien, 3; Neukirchen–Vluyn: Neukirchener Verlag, 1978).

subjectivity involved in detecting redactional activity (especially when it is identified in units as small as a colon). Nevertheless, his sensitivity to the flow of ideas within and especially between poems is instructive; it is this latter concern that places him alongside those scholars mentioned above.

P. Auffret has devoted considerable attention to structural studies, including three studies on collections in the Psalter (Psalms 15–24, 120–134, and 135–138).[1] His work on Psalms 120–134 differs considerably from Seybold's, since he is not concerned with redactional history but rather with existing surface structure. His method in elucidating the structures of the sections (especially Psalms 15–24) pays close attention to repeated words in both adjacent and non-adjacent psalms. The results generally show close (or at least logical) connections between adjacent psalms and significant connections between non-adjacent ones, as well. Often these latter connections contribute to the understanding of the structure of the entire section.

T. Collins's work is from a structuralist perspective.[2] As such, he considers the Psalter as an integrated system, in which the final work 'has something to say quite independent of the intentions of the authors of individual psalms, the collectors of groups of psalms or the editors of the psalter'.[3] For him, the Psalter's unity is at the implicit, subconscious level. This skepticism concerning the Psalter's ultimate meaning, that it does not reside even in the work of the final editors, sets Collins's work off from the work of most others above, despite the surface similarities.[4]

M.D. Goulder also has demonstrated interests that parallel those here, but that are somewhat different, in the last analysis.[5] At first glance, his work on Book IV is very similar to many of the above studies, since he stressed that the arrangement of psalms here was

---

1. These are collected in his *La sagesse a bâti sa maison: études de structures littéraires dans l'Ancient Testament et spécialement dans les psaumes* (OBO, 49; Göttingen: Vandenhoeck & Ruprecht, 1982).

2. T. Collins, 'Decoding the Psalms: A Structural Approach to the Psalter', *JSOT* 37 (1987), pp. 41-60.

3. Collins, 'Decoding the Psalms', p. 41.

4. He does not accept Wilson's arguments about editorial intentionality, for example (p. 58, n. 9).

5. Goulder, *The Psalms of the Sons of Korah*, and especially 'The Fourth Book of the Psalter'.

purposeful, that it was an 'ordered collection'.[1] He cited three features in support: (1) the presence of marked alternations in Book IV, in the form of repetitions of material especially among odd-numbered and even-numbered psalms, (2) the plausibility that this alternation was due to a pattern of morning and evening prayer, used over a period of eight days, likely at the Festival of Tabernacles and (3) given the second point, time references throughout Book IV suggest that the even-numbered psalms were intended for use in the evening.[2]

Goulder went on to propose a detailed liturgical setting for Book IV, associated with the fall Tabernacles Festival (the same one with which Mowinckel associated the 'Enthronement' Festival), complete with four motifs (the king, David and Solomon, Moses, YHWH) that tie the collection and the supposed Tabernacles liturgy together.[3] He then showed how each psalm in Book IV reflects one or more of these motifs.

There are two major differences between Goulder's essay and most of the works above. First, he saw a liturgical rationale for the final form of Book IV, whereas the others (except Seybold) have emphasized a literary one in the sections they have considered. There is no *necessary* conflict here, however, since most readily admit that the final form of the *Psalter* incorporated fixed sequences of originally liturgical material, the parade example being the psalms of ascents. Thus, hypothetically at least, a large liturgy such as Goulder postulated could have been incorporated undisturbed into the larger canonical corpus.

A second difference, however, is more problematic. Goulder paid minimal attention to links *within* the corpus he was analyzing, but rather focused on links between it and two other blocks of material, elsewhere in the canon, namely, 'the two great Tabernacles sagas, the J/E version of the Exodus and Desert traditions [Exodus 6–34] on the one side, and the Temple's foundation from 2 Sam. XXIV–I Kgs. IX on the other'.[4] He almost completely neglected any look at internal links within Book IV. Not only does this show Goulder's very different approach from the others; but it is also very doubtful that the many links between psalms in Book IV are so much owing to their use

1. Goulder, 'Fourth Book', pp. 269-70.
2. Goulder, 'Fourth Book', pp. 270-72.
3. Goulder, 'Fourth Book', pp. 274-75.
4. Goulder, 'Fourth Book', p. 274.

within the same festival and to their specific connections with another 'liturgy', and so little due to considerations of their similarities with each other.[1]

Finally, we should also note that some have been working on a lower level—that of connections between individual psalms. Much of Brennan's work is at this level.[2] W. Zimmerli[3] and C. Barth[4] also

---

1.   There are several other problems with Goulder's hypothesis, as well. (1) His assumption about an ordered collection does not rest upon three separate, independent supporting features, as he claimed (pp. 269-70), but rather on one undisputed feature—that of the alternation of subject matter between several odd- and even-numbered psalms—and on two that proceed from it. His second feature is a hypothesis, however plausible, deriving from the first, and does not support in its own right the idea of an ordered collection. The third feature derives from the second, and can be similarly judged. (2) Much weight is attached to the hypothesis that these are morning and evening readings. While this is certainly plausible in theory, Goulder's actual support for it is rather meager, limited to five references, only two of them even modestly clear, as he himself admitted (pp. 271-72). (3) The issue of its hypothetical nature must inevitably arise in this reconstruction. The comment of Childs with reference to the many attempts to reconstruct a lectionary cycle for the entire Psalter is appropriate here as well: 'Still the hypothetical nature of the various reconstructions along with sharp disagreement among the experts continues to pose serious problems and prevents anything resembling a consensus from emerging, even on basic issues' (B.S. Childs, 'Reflections on the Modern Study of the Psalms', in F.M. Cross, W.E. Lemke, P.D. Miller [eds.], *Magnalia Dei: The Mighty Acts of God* [Garden City, NY: Doubleday, 1976], p. 381). (4) In the same vein, as he reconstructed a proposed lectionary out of the two sagas, Goulder was forced to postulate lections of widely varying lengths (cf. the data in his Table on p. 286). For example, there are several rather short readings and other rather long ones in the same lection series. In Exodus, compare the following proposed lections: Exodus 6–9 [122 vv.] or Exodus 10–13 [112 vv.] with Exod. 14.1-22 [22 vv.] or Exodus 18 [27 vv.]; in Kings, compare 1 Kings 3 [28 vv.] or 1 Kings 7 [51 vv.] with 1 Kgs 6.1-13 [13 vv.] or 1 Kgs 8.65-9.9 [11 vv.]. Although this variety is found in several of the reconstructions of supposed lectionary cycles in the Psalter and the Pentateuch, it often appears to be a forced device to fit the scheme, rather than a natural one arising out of the texts. (See, for example, J.R. Porter, 'The Pentateuch and the Triennial Lectionary Cycle: An Examination of a Recent Theory', in F.F. Bruce (ed.), *Promise and Fulfillment* [Festschrift S.H. Hooke; Edinburgh: T. & T. Clark, 1963], pp. 163-74.)

2.   See above, p. 54 n. 1 and p. 57 n. 5.

3.   W. Zimmerli, 'Zwillingspsalmen', in J. Schreiner (ed.), *Wort, Lied, und Gottesspruch: Beiträge zu Psalmen und Propheten* (Festschrift J. Ziegler; Würzburg: Echter, 1972), pp. 105-13.

4.   C. Barth, 'Concatenatio im Ersten Buch des Psalters', in B. Benzing,

have contributed broadly focused essays on this level. Numerous scholars have worked on individual psalm pairs, as well.[1]

Zimmerli has focused on what he called 'twin psalms'. In all, he identified 40 'twin' psalms (20 pairs), and he did not pretend to be exhaustive. He began with the best known of the paired psalms—Psalms 9–10 and 42–43—and then noted the phenomenon of doublets, such as Psalms 14 and 53. Going beyond these obvious examples, however, he noted the principle of concatenation,[2] with and without key words (*Stichwörter*), in many places. Here he briefly noted connections of one sort or another between some 16 pairs of psalms.[3] The major portion of his article was devoted to developing in some detail the links between two other pairs—Psalms 111–112 and 105–106.[4] While much of what Zimmerli said is noted here and there in the commentaries, he made several original observations, particularly concerning the last two pairs; furthermore, his work is unique in naming the phenomenon and in specifically concentrating on it. He also emphasized that it is important to consider the editorial processes when reading individual psalms.[5]

C. Barth has made a systematic study of concatenation in one book of the Psalter. He first reviewed the work of scholars who had identified the phenomenon, beginning with Delitzsch, and those who have disputed it.[6] Then he listed the repeated roots between each adjacent pair of psalms in Book I, including those between several non-

---

O. Böcher, G. Mayer (eds.), *Wort und Wirklichkeit: Studien zur afrikanistik und orientalistik* (Festschrift E.L. Rapp; Meisenheim am Glan: Hain, 1976), pp. 30-40.

1. Recent works that focus on individual pairs of psalms include the following: L.C. Allen, 'David as Exemplar of Spirituality: The Redactional Function of Psalm 19', *Bib* 67 (1986), pp. 544-46; P. Auffret, 'Essai sur la structure littéraire du Psaume 94', *Biblische Notizen* 24 (1984), pp. 44-72; 'Complements sur la structure littéraire du Ps 2 et son rapport au Ps 1', *Biblische Notizen* 35 (1986), pp. 7-13; J.K. Kuntz, 'King Triumphant: A Rhetorical Study of Psalms 20 and 21', *HAR* 10 (1986), pp. 157-76; J.L. Mays, 'The Place of the Torah-Psalms in the Psalter', *JBL* 106 (1987), pp. 3-12 (10-11).

2. Without specifically mentioning the term.

3. Zimmerli, 'Zwillingspsalmen', p. 106. These texts are Psalms 1–2, 3–4, 30–31, 31–32, 32–33, 38–39, 39–40, 40–41, 43–44, 69–70, 73–74, 74–75, 77–78, 79–80, 80–81, and 127–128.

4. Zimmerli, 'Zwillingspsalmen', pp. 107-11.

5. Zimmerli, 'Zwillingspsalmen', pp. 105, 111.

6. Barth, 'Concatenatio', pp. 30-32.

adjacent psalms.[1] Out of the data thus collected, he listed 17 principles of concatenation, including exact recurrences of forms (including affixes), recurrences of roots, recurrences of word-pairs (and even three- and four-word sequences).[2] Sometimes these have structural significance, as well, as when the key words occur at the beginning of one psalm and at the end of the next (or vice versa). He even noted that text-critical work yields even more examples of the phenomenon than are visible in the MT alone. He conceded that not all of the examples are equally strong but, all in all, his is a valuable contribution.

Conclusion

The above survey shows that most studies on the question of editorial activity in the Psalter approach it either at the higher level of collections and large, organizing principles, or at the lower level of links between adjacent psalms, and some do so at both levels. The work at the higher level is valuable in setting the framework within which more detailed work can proceed. Here, sapiential and royal motifs can be seen most clearly.

At the lower level, the work functions to provide more specific evidence and to confirm or modify the higher-level investigations. Here, links of various types may be seen, and specific royal or wisdom contours are not as visible, but they do appear. It should be obvious that, if work at the lower level continues very long, soon every pair of adjacent psalms will be shown to have some significant—or logical—links between them, and a pattern of purposeful editorial activity will emerge at the lowest levels, alongside the patterns already demonstrated at the higher levels.

Much work remains to be done at both levels. On the higher level, works such as Reindl's, Westermann's and Wilson's need to be extended, tested and refined. Wilson's is especially significant and much fruitful work could be done in testing and applying his suggestions. On the lower level, each psalm pair needs to be explored in this light, in more detail than did early commentators such as Delitzsch and Alexander.

The current focus on unitary, literary or 'canonical' readings of all portions of the Bible is bringing much new information to light about

1.   Barth, 'Concatenatio', pp. 32-35.
2.   Barth, 'Concatenatio', pp. 35-40.

the messages and intents of the ancient authors, and these studies in the Psalter are beginning to do so, as well. The reading of individual psalms can only be enhanced when these are considered in light of their neighboring psalms, and the reading of the Psalter as a whole is likewise enhanced when its larger themes are highlighted.

Postscript (May 1991)

The above essay, completed in early 1988, surveyed the literature through 1987. In the interim, interest in the Psalter's editorial processes has continued.

Most worthy of note is the establishment of the Psalms Group in the Society of Biblical Literature, which has devoted a significant portion of its early sessions to the topic at hand: witness the work in the present volume.

Outside of this volume, several other works merit attention. D. Grossberg has studied several poetic corpora as coherent but multivalent collections (the psalms of ascents, the Song of Songs and Lamentations).[1] Grossberg sees various literary forces at work in opposite directions in these sections, forces that emphasize both the unity and diversity in them.

A.R. Ceresko has provided a survey of the sage in the Psalms, on three levels: (1) the wise man is pictured in the Psalms as one who prays and observes Torah, (2) the sages were authors of several psalms, in which they revealed their special concerns for wisdom and order, (3) a sage (or sages) was responsible for the formation and shape of the Psalter itself, and, as such, was the 'author' of the Psalter.[2] Ceresko develops this last point[3] to emphasize the self-conscious authorial activity behind the collection process, one which displays 'a unity intentionally greater than its parts'.[4] The scholar-

---

1. D. Grossberg, *Centripetal and Centrifugal Structures in Biblical Poetry* (SBLMS, 39; Atlanta: Scholars Press, 1989); see pp. 15-54 on the psalms of ascents.

2. A.R. Ceresko, 'The Sage in the Psalms', in J.G. Gammie and L.G. Perdue (eds.), *The Sage in Israel and the Ancient Near East* (Winona Lake, IN: Eisenbrauns, 1990), pp. 217-30.

3. Drawing upon B.L. Mack, *Wisdom and the Hebrew Epic: Ben-Sira's Hymn in Praise of the Fathers* (Chicago: University of Chicago Press, 1985).

4. Ceresko, 'The Sage', p. 230.

sage, as one who prays, was a fitting author of the Psalter, the collection par excellence of Israel's prayers.

M.E. Tate's commentary on Psalms 51–100 evidences special interest in the editorial shape and shaping of the Psalter.[1] He has drawn from Wilson's work in speaking of several over-arching themes in the collections, and he also displays a sensitivity to inter-psalm relationships and links.

J.H. Walton has attempted to see in the Psalter a 'cantata' (that is, independent compositions woven together into a secondary framework) organized around the theme of the Davidic Covenant.[2] He sees Book I addressing 'David's Conflict with Saul'; Book II, 'David's Reign'; Book III, 'Assyrian Crisis'; Book IV, 'Introspection about Destruction of Temple and Exile' and Book V, 'Praise/Reflection on Return and New Era'. Walton's work is highly original, his focus upon the Davidic Covenant is well taken, and he presents some intriguing possibilities. However, his orientation is somewhat akin to Goulder's, in seeking links to canonical collections outside the Psalter, and, as such, some of the criticisms of Goulder noted above would apply to Walton, as well. Indeed, his work is far more wide-ranging than Goulder's, and thus even less amenable to controls, and it appears to be even more arbitrary than Goulder's at several points. At the very least, the hypothesis needs careful and extensive testing.

P. Auffret continues his prolific output of structural studies, and occasionally devotes attention to inter-psalm links, as well.[3]

Finally, a morphologically and syntactically tagged version of the Hebrew Bible is now available for computer use—the Westminster Hebrew Text. A comprehensive study of the entire Psalter's vocabulary is now within easy reach, with the possibility of showing which lexical repetitions between any two psalms—and within and among groupings of psalms—are merely random and which are significant. Now the studies at the lowest levels of analysis should be able to give much more precise correlation to the studies at the higher levels.[4]

---

1.   M.E. Tate, *Psalms 51–100* (WBC, 20; Waco, TX: Word Books, 1990).

2.   J.H. Walton, 'Psalms: A Cantata About the Davidic Covenant', *JETS* 34 (1991), pp. 21-31.

3.   For example, ' "Allez, fils, entendez-moi": étude structurelle du Psaume 34 et son rapport au Psaume 33', *Eglise et Théologie* 19 (1988), pp. 5-31.

4.   See the excursus in my essay in the present volume ('A Contextual Reading of Psalms 90–94') for a rudimentary attempt at this type of analysis.

Part II

THE PSALTER: A WHOLE AND ITS PARTS

SHAPING THE PSALTER: A CONSIDERATION OF EDITORIAL LINKAGE IN THE BOOK OF PSALMS

Gerald H. Wilson

It has become popular in many circles to refer to the Psalter as a 'hymnbook'—a collection of individual compositions created for performance in the worship of ancient Israel. While there is a certain appropriateness to such a claim, it remains, in my opinion, an unhappy characterization for several reasons. First, the hymnbook analogy ignores the fact that, in the final analysis, the canonical Psalter has become a book to be read and meditated upon (Psalm 1), rather than music to be sung. Secondly, the designation evidences our tendency over the last 150 years of Psalms study to focus almost exclusively on individual psalms to the neglect of the whole ensemble.

Recent scholarship has suggested there is more to the arrangement of the Psalms than has hitherto met the eye. It now seems established beyond doubt that the Psalter as a whole has been subjected to a unifying editorial process resulting in the five-book structure and other evidence of theological and literary shaping of the materials. We begin by reviewing the more significant recent insights into the editorial shaping of the Psalter.

The Five-Book Division of the Psalter

Recent research has confirmed the five-book division of the Psalter (marked off by a series of doxologies) as a purposeful indication of editorial organization. The reality of these divisions is confirmed in the first three books (Psalms 2–89) not only by the doxologies present at the ends of these divisions, but also by the consistent change of both author and genre designations in the psalm-headings at precisely these same points of disjuncture. Elsewhere author and genre designations are employed to link together groups of psalms and to smooth the transition between them.[1] Additional confirmation is found in the placement of 'royal psalms' at three of the four critical points of juncture marking the boundaries of the first three books (Psalms 2, 72, 89). The absence of a fourth royal psalm at the end of Book I (Psalm 41) may be explained by the earlier combination of Books I and II into a unified collection of Davidic hymns as indicated by the postscript in 72.20.[2]

Two Distinct Segments of the Psalter

It has also been demonstrated that the first three books employ very different organizational techniques than the last two (Psalms 90–150) and that these two segments have likely experienced separate histories of transmission. In the first three books, author and genre designations in the psalm-headings are utilized editorially to group psalms together and to indicate divisions between such groupings. In the later books, where such designations are largely lacking, *hllwyh* psalms (or groups of such psalms) regularly mark the conclusion of segments while *hwdw* psalms (those beginning with *hwdw lyhwh ky ṭwb ky l'wlm ḥsdw*) begin subsequent sections. These clearly distinct principles of editorial arrangement, coupled with the apparent lack of concern to place 'royal psalms' at the seams of the last two books, suggest the probability of two distinct periods of editorial activity behind these segments.[3]

Evidence for the arrangement of the psalms from the Qumran manuscripts brings additional light to the subject. While the Qumran psalms manuscripts at points yield evidence of considerable variation from the arrangement and contents of the canonical Psalter, variation is practically non-existent in the first three books. By contrast, extensive variations in order and content occur in the last two books. When this evidence of variation is correlated with the age of the manuscripts in which it occurs, variation is consistently associated with earlier manuscripts while later manuscripts (beginning about CE 50) regularly conform to the canonical arrangement. So, the Qumran evidence

1. G.H. Wilson, 'Evidence of Editorial Divisions in the Hebrew Psalter', *VT* 34 (1984), pp. 337-52.
2. G.H. Wilson, 'The Use of Royal Psalms at the "Seams" of the Hebrew Psalter', *JSOT* 35 (1986), pp. 85-94.
3. Wilson, 'Evidence of Editorial Divisions', pp. 337-52.

confirms two distinct segments of the Psalter and suggests further that Books I–III were already fixed while Books IV–V were still in a state of flux.[1]

An Introduction and a Conclusion

Further indication of a unified editorial process shaping the Psalter is found in the general recognition that Psalm 1 has been appended to the Psalter as a hermeneutical introduction.[2] This psalm provides the interpretive context from which to see the psalms not only as human cries to God (although they mirror that eloquently!), but as a source of divine communication to humans. It stresses private, individual meditation as an important mode of access to the theological message of the psalms and, in so doing, shifts the function of these compositions away from public, communal cultic performance.

At the other end of the Psalter the final collection concludes with the exalted praise of the final *hallel* in Psalms 146–150. The lack of any concluding doxology at the end of the fifth book suggests this group of *hllwyh* psalms provides the necessary closure of the last book and, indeed, of the whole Psalter. This resounding praise is consciously set in motion by David's words in Ps. 145.21 ('My mouth will speak the praise of YHWH, and let all flesh bless his holy name for ever and ever'). The resulting crescendo of praise swells until in 150.6 'everything that has breath' joins together in the concluding hallelujah.[3] This apparent concern to provide hermeneutical perspective and a sense of closure in the Psalter lends credence to an editorial process of arrangement that extends to the whole book, from beginning to end.

A Series of Editorial 'Frames'

I have discussed in another forum and in some detail how the placement of royal psalms at the 'seams' of the combined collection of Books I

---

1.   G.H. Wilson, 'The Qumran Psalms Manuscripts and the Consecutive Arrangement of Psalms in the Hebrew Psalter', *CBQ* 45 (1983), pp. 377-88.

2.   For a recent summary of the discussion see B.S. Childs, *Introduction to the Old Testament as Scripture* (Philadelphia: Fortress Press, 1979), pp. 513-14.

3.   G.H. Wilson, *The Editing of the Hebrew Psalter* (SBLDS, 76; Chico, CA: Scholars Press, 1985), pp. 189-90, 225-28.

through III (Psalms 2–89) provides an interpretive context for this segment of the Psalter.[1] The framework focuses the concern of those frustrated by the apparent failure of the Davidic covenant and kingdom, and it articulates their continuing appeal to God for redress and restoration. I have also suggested that the last two books (Psalms 90–150) respond to the problem raised by the first three and seek to offer a new perspective and theological resolution.[2] I would now like to explore how a further series of editorial frames have been employed to structure the whole Psalter and to bind all its diverse units into a cohesive unity.

a. *Book IV (Psalms 90–106)*

As one moves from the first three books into the fourth, a shift is immediately observed. Here untitled psalms predominate. Only seven of these 17 psalms have titles at all; and only three of these name an author (Moses in Psalm 90 and David in Psalms 101, 103). The preponderance of untitled psalms would have afforded the editor a degree of flexibility in arrangement unheard of in the first three books where author designations are the rule. It is not surprising, therefore, to find here a sustained, thematic unity that focuses on the kingship of YHWH.

The fourth book contains two major blocks of psalms—the YHWH-*mālak* psalms (93, 96–99) and the Davidic collection (101, 103–104). In his recent PhD dissertation,[3] David M. Howard, Jr investigated the arrangement of Psalms 93–100 and discovered (among other things) that Psalms 95 and 100 form a 'frame' around the core YHWH-*mālak* group (96–99). He is somewhat at a loss to explain the separation of Psalm 93 from this core group to which it is obviously related. Had he extended his study to include the whole of the fourth book, he would have noticed how the interchange of Psalms 93 and 94 provides an interlocking mechanism by which the YHWH-*mālak* group (with its 'frame') is bound together with the preceding group of Psalms 90–92 and 94.

This introductory group of psalms hangs together around a common theme that I have chosen to call 'Mosaic' (because of the title of Psalm

1. Wilson, 'The Use of Royal Psalms', pp. 85-94.
2. Wilson, *Editing*, pp. 214-28; see also my article, 'A First Century CE Date for the Closing of the Hebrew Psalter?' in *Haim M. I. Gevaryahu Memorial Volume* (Jerusalem: World Jewish Bible Center, 1990), pp. 136-43.
3. D.M. Howard, Jr, 'The Structure of Psalms *93–100*' (PhD dissertation, University of Michigan, Ann Arbor, 1986).

90, the use of the old divine names El Shadday and El Elyon, references to Moses and Aaron, the Exodus wanderings and other thematic correspondences). These psalms emphasize a 'pre-monarchic' reliance on YHWH alone that exalts God's wondrous, eternal works in contrast to the weak and transitory nature of humanity. Rather than encouraging confidence in human rulers, these psalms counsel the hearer to find refuge in YHWH who alone is eternal and able to save. These themes provide an appropriate introduction to the central YHWH-*mālak* psalms that celebrate the kingship of YHWH.

Psalms 90–92 and 94 share numerous verbal and thematic connections with the concluding psalms of Book IV (105–106). Together these psalms form a 'Mosaic frame' that provides an interpretive *entrée* to the book and in the process binds together the YHWH-*mālak* psalms and the Davidic collection into a unified whole. Thorough analysis of the significance of the final arrangement must await another time, but I have dealt with the subject briefly on another occasion.[1]

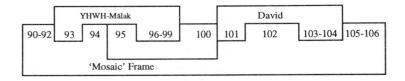

Figure a. *Book IV*

This investigation into the structure of the fourth book has uncovered two editorial techniques of organization that will be useful as we consider the rest of the Psalter—the 'overlap/interlock' technique for binding groups together and the 'frame' that provides an interpretive context.

b. *Books II and III (Psalms 42/3–89)*

As mentioned previously, one important organizational element in the first three books is author designation. These two books provide us with four major collections: Davidic—Psalms 51–72 and 86; Asaphite—Psalms 50, 73–83; and two Qorahite—Psalms 42/3–49, 84–85 and 87–88.

Drawing on our study of Book IV, the isolated Davidic Psalm 86

---

1.   Wilson, *Editing*, pp. 214-19.

and the 'orphan' Asaphite Psalm 50 can be seen to perform a similar binding/locking function as observed with Psalms 93 and 94. In addition, the whole book has been provided with a 'Qorahite frame' that both introduces and concludes it. In this final combination, the Davidic Psalm 86 constitutes an additional tether binding the latter Qorahite group to the whole. This may relate to the fact that the Elohistic Psalter concludes at Psalm 83 and this latter Qorahite group (84–85, 87–88) is of distinct character (and perhaps distinct origin) from the earlier group and needs clearly to be bound in.

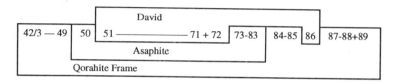

Figure b. *Books II and III*

c. *Book I (Psalms 3–41)*
The postscript at 72.20 ('The prayers of David, son of Jesse, are ended') plus the lack of a royal psalm at the junction of Books I and II (Psalm 41), might indicate that at some point in the development of the Psalter parts of Books I and II were combined into a Davidic collection terminating with the postscript in 72.20. If this is so, then the third book (Psalms 73–89) would have been appended subsequently. The recognition of the existence of a distinctively Elohistic Psalter (Psalms 42–83) that includes the interwoven Davidic and Asaphite collection (50–83) along with the first Qorahite group (42–49) complicates the issue, however. The anomalous character of both Psalms 72 and 89 within their respective contexts (see below), suggests alternatively that Psalm 72, with its doxology and postscript, may be a later editorial intrusion that has disturbed the original integrity of the Elohistic Psalter. My purpose at this point is to describe the final shape of the Psalter rather than the process by which it assumed that shape. These difficulties, while important and intriguing, are not ultimately decisive for my discussion.

Extension of the growing structure of Books II and III to include Book I results in a sophisticated interweaving of these groupings. The Qorahite frame that dominated the combined Books II and III is now offset by a heavily Davidic introductory collection (3–41). But, looking at the whole of the combined first three books, an additional editorial framework becomes apparent. This framework is provided by the placement of royal psalms at the seams of these books as previously mentioned.

Psalm 2 stands aloof from its context as an untitled psalm at the beginning of the Davidic collection. Psalm 72 at the end of Book II is linked to the preceding Davidic collection by its Solomonic title, the initial mention of 'the king...and the king's son' in 72.1, and the postscript indicating the end of 'the prayers of David...' in 72.20. Yet it remains aloof and anomalous because of its designation to Solomon.

Psalm 89 is linked to the final Qorahite Psalm 88 in an unusual way. Psalm 88 bears a dual heading: *libnê qōrah...maśkîl lĕhêmān hā'ezrāḥî*. The heading of Psalm 89 is related to this last element since it too is a *maśkîl lĕ'ētān hā'ezrāḥî*. The result is that Psalm 89 is also linked to its context and yet aloof from it. The fact that each of these three psalms is (a) a royal psalm, (b) at a seam of a book, (c) somewhat aloof from its immediate context, and (d) bound secondarily into its context, lends support to my contention that they have been so placed in order to provide editorial shape to the combined collection.

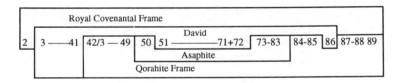

Figure c. *Books I to III*

These three psalms form a covenantal frame around the first three books. As I have shown elsewhere,[1] this frame is concerned with the institution (Psalm 2), the transmission (Psalm 72), and the failure (Psalm 89) of the Davidic covenant.

d. *Book V (Psalms 107–145)*
This leaves us with the task of incorporating the final book of the Psalter into this growing structure (considering Psalms 146–150 as a conclusion to the fifth book and the whole Psalter). The fifth book is possibly the most diverse and difficult to sort out, partially because

---

1. Wilson, 'The Use of Royal Psalms', pp. 85-94.

there are so few roadsigns and landmarks in these predominantly untitled psalms. There are three major segments marked out by *hwdw* introductions and *hllwyh* conclusions, namely, Psalms 107–117 (a first Davidic group); Psalms 118–135 (which frame Psalm 119 and Psalms 120–134, the songs of ascents); Psalms 136–145 (a second Davidic group).[1] The positioning of these three segments provides a collection characterized by a Davidic frame and a center focused on the massive acrostic Psalm 119. I have yet to work out the significance of this arrangement to my complete satisfaction, but see my tentative comments elsewhere.[2]

One further observation about this collection deserves comment before I proceed to the question of the whole Psalter. When one considers the beginning and concluding psalms of this grouping (107 and 145), it becomes immediately clear that we are dealing with an additional 'wisdom frame' around this group of psalms. While on the whole Psalm 107 is not what one might identify as a wisdom psalm, it does conclude in 107.42-43 on a clear wisdom note: 'the upright see it and are glad; and all wickedness stops its mouth. Whoever is wise, let him give heed to these things, let men consider the steadfast love of YHWH.'

At the other end of the book, Psalm 145 presents a further wisdom challenge. This acrostic psalm extols the kingship of YHWH and God's love, and it concludes in 145.19-20 with the wisdom admonition: 'He fulfills the desire of all who fear him, he also hears their cry, and saves them. YHWH preserves all who love him, but all the wicked he will destroy.'

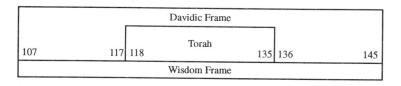

Figure d. *Book V*

e. *Books IV and V (Psalms 90–145)*
This wisdom frame in Book V provides us with the unifying element that draws together Books IV and V as well. Book IV begins with a

---

1. Wilson, 'Evidence of Editorial Divisions', pp. 349-52.
2. Wilson, *Editing*, pp. 220-28.

psalm that reflects (at least in part) the concerns of the wisdom tradition. Psalm 90 contrasts the sovereignty of God with the transience of humanity and offers its own explicit wisdom teaching in 90.11-12. 'Who considers the power of your anger and your wrath according to the fear of you? So teach us to number our days, that we may get a heart of wisdom.' In addition, Psalm 91, which in some traditions has been connected with 90, has also been described as a wisdom psalm. This recognition allows us to extend the wisdom frame to include Book IV.

f. *The Final Frame*
If what I have said so far were all that there was to say, then we would have delineated two distinct segments of the Psalter—one (Psalms 2–89) characterized by a 'Royal Covenantal Frame', the other (Psalms 90–145) shaped by the concerns of wisdom. But there is further evidence that these two segments have been editorially bound together into a whole.

The first element of note is the extension of the Royal Covenantal Frame by the placement of Psalm 144 toward the end of the fifth book. In this final royal psalm, David, in themes reminiscent of the central YHWH-*mālak* psalms in Book IV, praises YHWH as his fortress, stronghold, deliverer and calls on God for rescue. The psalm concludes with the wisdom blessing (*'ašrê*), 'Happy are the people whose God is YHWH'. This provides a fitting counter to the rebellious nations who reject YHWH in Psalm 2. Psalm 144 resounds throughout with echoes of the concluding admonition of Psalm 2, 'Happy [*'ašrê*] are all who take *refuge* in him [YHWH]'.

At the same time, the placement of the Psalm 1 as introduction extends the wisdom frame to embrace the whole Psalter. It is instructive that as Psalm 1 begins the Psalter with an exposition of the 'two ways' and counsels the reader to follow the way known by YHWH rather than the way of perishing, so Psalm 145 concludes the Psalter on a similar note. In 145.19-20, the psalmist describes the same tension between the righteous and the wicked when he says: 'YHWH preserves all who love him; but all the wicked he will destroy'. So, as the wisdom blessing at the end of 144.15 parallels the similar blessing at the end of Ps. 2.12, these two descriptions of the conflicting ways of life and death balance the beginning and ending of the Psalter and support the reality of a final wisdom frame. Confirmation of the existence of this framework is further strengthened by the realization that even the third book opens with a wisdom psalm, Psalm 73.

In the final analysis, the shape of the canonical Psalter preserves a tense dialogue (or a dialogue in tension) between the royal covenantal hopes associated with the first two-thirds of the Psalter and the wisdom counsel to trust YHWH alone associated with the final third. In conclusion it seems apparent that wisdom has had the last word as demonstrated by the wisdom shaping of the covenantal Psalms 2 and 144 as well as the primary positioning of Psalms 1 and 145 in the final frame.

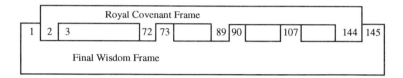

Figure e. *The Final Frame*

In an interesting (and perhaps related) movement noted by many,[1] the Psalter begins with an emphasis on private, individual lamentation, but concludes with public, communal proclamation of praise. It is between these two poles of human experience and access to God that the continuing life of the faithful is to be lived out. Are the final editors seeking to counter the lamentation associated with the collapse of the Davidic hopes in the first three books with a call to praise the only true and eternal King—Israel's only hope? As a result of its final form, the Psalter counters continuing concern for the restoration of the Davidic dynasty and kingdom with the wise counsel to seek refuge in a kingdom 'not of this world'—the eternal kingdom in which YHWH alone is king. I began with the common predilection to proclaim the Psalter the 'hymnbook' of the Second Temple. Both the clear evidence of organization evident in the book, and the apparent shift of function away from public performance to private meditation and appropriation, render 'hymnbook' an inadequate and misleading designation. If I were to choose a happier musical metaphor, I would

1.   N.K. Gottwald, *The Hebrew Bible: A Socio-literary Introduction* (Philadelphia: Fortress Press, 1985), p. 535; K. Seybold, *Introducing the Psalms* (Edinburgh: T. & T. Clark, 1990), pp. 26-28.

prefer 'the musical score', with its ability to bring together a diversity of instruments and patterns of notes into proper timing and thus into a harmonious whole that exceeds the sum of its parts. Rather than a hymnbook, the Psalter is a symphony with many movements, or better yet an oratorio in which a multitude of voices—singly and in concert—rise in a crescendo of praise. While each individual composition may stand on its own—as an aria from the *Elijah*—the whole has an integrity that cannot and must not be ignored.

THE BEGINNING OF THE PSALTER

Patrick D. Miller

The beginning and end of a book are among the chief indicators of its subject matter. That is not always true of biblical books, but it is of some. In straightforward language, Deut. 1.1-5 sets forth the intention of the book to declare the words of Moses at a particular time and place and understands these words as an exposition of the Torah. The rest of the book then sets forth those words and that exposition as Moses' speech on the plain. Chapter 34 is less clear in this regard but is certainly an ending to the Mosaic words. Its focus is more upon Moses than it is upon the Torah that is the primary substance of the book. But its character as an ending to the book is obvious. The book of Job begins in story fashion but sets the stage as a beginning should do, and its ending wraps things up in story fashion. While Proverbs is a motley collection of sayings without much unity, it is given a dual introduction, one part identifying the content of the book as the Proverbs of Solomon (1.1) and the other giving a substantive introduction to the material that follows (vv. 2-6). The beginning and ending of Qohelet serve quite definitely as introduction and wrap-up, reflecting in their different content the dual perspectives of the book, the sense of the vanity of existence and the responsibility to fear God. The prophetic books commonly have introductions, usually brief superscriptions setting time and place and identifying the prophet to whom the following oracles are ascribed. Sometimes the introduction is more extended, as, for example, in the case of Jeremiah, where the call story sets the agenda of the book in large fashion (Jer. 1.10).[1] The endings of the prophetic books are less clearly conclusions to the book

---

1. Note how W. Brueggemann has recently entitled his two-volume commentary on Jeremiah with lines from this verse: *Jeremiah 1–25: To Pluck Up, To Tear Down* and *Jeremiah 26–52: To Build, To Plant* (International Theological Commentary; Grand Rapids: Eerdmans, 1988 and 1991).

that wrap them up in some fashion, though there are several where the exposition of the book could and sometimes does identify such a function in the final chapter or verses. What is often true of the prophetic books is that in some fashion they carry things forward, usually in what are recognized as salvation or eschatological oracles, anticipating the redemptive grace of God beyond judgment. Lamentations would seem to be one of the books without introduction or conclusion, but that is not quite the case. The opening verses identify the primary subject of these laments, the destruction and ruin of Jerusalem, and the ending verses (Lam. 5.20-22) give the fundamental question raised by that destruction and one to which the prophets of the exile, such as Deutero-Isaiah, seek to respond.

The Psalter seems less clearly to have an introduction and a conclusion, but in fact, like Lamentations, while it simply starts off with a psalm and ends with another one, there is a definite introduction, as many have recognized, and a less clear but meaningful conclusion. In this essay, I wish to explore the way in which the beginning of the Psalter opens up the subject matter not only of the Psalms as a whole but particularly of the first book of the Psalter (Psalms 3–41), so that it functions as a kind of dual introduction of the first part and then of the whole.

The function of Psalm 1 as an introduction to the Psalter has been recognized and discussed, especially in recent literature on the Psalms.[1] The relation of Psalm 2 to Psalm 1, however, and its role vis-à-vis the introduction to the Psalter is a matter of debate. Some have suggested that the two psalms may have been a single composition, indicated especially by (1) the lack of a superscription before Psalm 2, the only psalm in Book I of the Psalter without one except for Psalms 10 and 33, which are linked to the two preceding psalms; (2) the *'ašrê* clauses at the beginning of Psalm 1 and the end of Psalm 2 acting as an inclusion unifying the two compositions; and (3) the

---

1.   See P. Auffret, *The Literary Structure of Psalm 2* (JSOTSup, 3; Sheffield: JSOT Press, 1977); G.H. Wilson, *The Editing of the Hebrew Psalter* (SBLDS, 76; Chico, CA: Scholars Press, 1985), pp. 204-207; P.D. Miller, *Interpreting the Psalms* (Philadelphia: Fortress Press, 1986), pp. 81-88; G. Sheppard, *Wisdom as a Hermeneutical Construct* (BZAW, 151; Berlin: de Gruyter, 1980), pp. 136-44; J. Reindl, 'Weisheitliche Bearbeitung von Psalmen: Ein Beitrag zum Verständnis der Sammlung des Psalters', in J.A. Emerton (ed.), *Congress Volume, Vienna 1980* (VTSup, 32; Leiden: Brill, 1981), pp. 333-56.

various linguistic connections between the two psalms.[1] Whether or not one should see the Psalms as originally a single composition—and there are obvious reasons for regarding them as separate and distinct psalms[2]—the connections between the two are undeniable. They indicate, at least on the editing level, that Psalms 1 and 2 were to be read together as an *entrée* into the Psalter. It may have been that Psalm 2 was originally the first psalm of the Psalter,[3] to which Psalm 1 was later added as an introduction to the whole; but now they stand closely together as a single, if complex, way into the psalms that follow.

In two particular ways, Psalm 1 sets the agenda for the Psalter, but more particularly for the first book of Psalms (Psalms 3–41). One of these is the identification of the way of the wicked and the way of the righteous as well as their respective fates. These two categories of people dominate the psalms. There is some sense in which human community is broken up into these two groups, though at times they are given other names, such as fool and wise, or evil-doers and those who fear the Lord. But how these two groups act, the way they go— whether one means their path of life or their ultimate fate—is very much the subject matter of the psalms.

That is especially so for the first book of the Psalms. Nearly half of the references to the 'wicked' after Psalm 1–2 are in the next 39 psalms. The figures are slightly less balanced with regard to the 'righteous', Psalms 3–41 having 26 references, and the rest of the Psalter 37. But the focus on these two groups is marked.

That focus is further reflected in the dominance of the prayers for help or laments in the first book of the Psalter, for it is especially in these psalms that both the wicked and the righteous come to the fore. The righteous are referred to less often than the wicked, in part because it is their voice that speaks in these laments. *ṣaddîq* is not simply 'righteous' in a moral sense; it is also the innocent in a social context. Or it is the case that in these prayers, the morally righteous are those innocent victims falsely accused, shamed, oppressed and afflicted. In the case of one of the psalms in Book I, Psalm 37, we have the most extensive discourse on the relation of the wicked and the righteous and their two ways outside of Psalm 1. In general, the plight of the victim,

1.   See especially Auffret, *The Literary Structure of Psalm 2*.

2.   See J. Willis, 'Psalm 1—An Entity', *ZAW* 9 (1979), pp. 381-401. His arguments are approvingly summarized in Wilson, *Editing*, pp. 205-206.

3.   On this, see Wilson, *Editing*, p. 204.

the *ṣaddîq*, in the face of the wicked is very much to the fore at the beginning of the Psalter and throughout much of Book I. And the harsh fate of the wicked at the hands of a righteous God is a matter of constant observation (e.g. 3.6; 5.5-7; 7.10).

The other way in which themes of the first book of the Psalter unfold in the introductory Psalm 1 is in its emphasis on the Torah, the joy of studying it, and its positive benefits for those who do. At one time, this psalm may have formed an inclusion with Psalm 119, which would have ended the Psalter echoing the basic notes sounded in Psalm 1.[1] Apart from Psalm 119, however, the primary emphases on the Torah are found explicitly and implicitly in the first book. Psalm 19 is the most direct reflection of Psalm 1, as it spells out in great detail the positive character of the Torah and its benefits for those who study and keep it. But the focus on the Torah is found also in the entrance liturgies of Psalms 15 and 24. The answers to the questions asked of those seeking entrance into the holy place reflect a number of stipulations of the Torah.[2] It has been proposed that Psalms 15–24 form a particular group of psalms arranged in a ring structure of which Psalms 15 and 24 are the outer ring or inclusion and Psalm 19 the center.[3] If such a proposal has any merit, it places at the center of Book I of the Psalter a group of psalms with a particular focus on obedience to and delight in the Torah of the Lord.

The one other place in the Psalter where 'delight' *ḥpṣ* (cf. Ps. 1.2) is expressed in the will, that is, the Torah of the Lord is in Ps. 40.8-9, the next-to-last psalm of Book I. The psalmist in this context offers himself or herself as one who conforms to the model set forth in Psalm 1:

> Then I said, 'Here I am;
> in the scroll of the book it is written of me.
> I delight to do your will, O my God;
> your law is within my heart' (NRSV).

---

1. See C. Westermann, *Praise and Lament in the Psalms* (trans. K.R. Crim and R.N. Soulen; Atlanta: John Knox, 1981), p. 253.

2. See K. Koch, 'Tempeleinlassliturgien und Dekaloge', in R. Rendtorff and K. Koch (eds.), *Studien zur theologie der alttestamentlichen Überlieferungen* (Neukirchen–Vluyn: Neukirchener Verlag, 1961), pp. 45-60.

3. P. Auffret, *La sagesse a bâti sa maison* (OBO, 49; Göttingen: Vandenhoeck & Ruprecht, 1982), pp. 407-38. In this understanding of the arrangement, Psalms 16 and 23 are balancing songs of trust, Psalms 17 and 22 are balancing laments, and 18 and 20–21 are balancing royal psalms.

The 'introduction' or 'prologue' to the Psalter, and more particularly to the first book of the Psalter,[1] however, now includes Psalm 2. It too points directions for the reading and understanding of the psalms that follow. That happens in several ways. Most generally, it moves the plane of subject matter onto the world of nations and rulers. It is not simply the individual Torah-adherent who speaks in these psalms, and the groups who are present in one way or another are not simply the wicked and the righteous. The king or ruler also speaks and is spoken of in the psalms, and the groups who operate within its sphere include nations and rulers. The wicked whose way perishes at the end of Psalm 1 are echoed in the warning to the kings and rulers at the end of Psalm 2 lest they 'perish in the way'.

The most direct way in which we discern the subject matter of Psalm 2 being picked up in the first book of the Psalter is in the presence of three royal psalms within its limits. Whereas there are other royal psalms in the Psalter, these three quite specifically reflect the kind of circumstance envisioned in Psalm 2, the king under threat or attack. One of the royal psalms in Book I is a prayer for the king before battle (Psalm 20). The other two give thanks for God's protection and victory against the enemies of the Lord's anointed (Psalms 18 and 21). As Psalm 2 identifies the threat of the rulers who 'take counsel together against the Lord and his anointed' and notes that the one 'who sits in the heavens laughs', so 'David' echoes that confidence in Psalm 20:

> Now I know that the Lord will help his anointed;
> he will answer him from his holy heaven
> with mighty victories by his right hand (v. 7; NRSV).

Psalm 2, in effect, sets the stage upon which it is possible to pray the prayers and give the thanks that Psalms 18, 20 and 21 express. It is not just a matter of having a royal psalm at the beginning of the Psalter. It is this particular one that leads us into what follows and lays

1. We are not making any effort to decide at what redactional stage Psalms 1 and 2 were added to the beginning of the Psalter as an introduction. As Sheppard has noted, this combined prologue may have been added at the latest stage in the redactional history of the Psalter or to an earlier smaller collection ending with either Psalm 119 or Psalm 41. Once the redactional move has been made, the introductory function works on all levels. We are attempting to show how that is particularly the case with the first book of the Psalter without assuming necessarily that the Prologue was added at that point or is to be confined to that book in its function. See Sheppard, *Wisdom as a Hermeneutical Construct*, p. 142.

the ground for other psalms by and about the king. Further, as Gerald Wilson has noted, Psalm 2 'finds echoes in the concerns of Psalm 41, which concludes the first book. There David as the author speaks of the assurance of YHWH's protection and security in the face of the malicious murmuring of his enemies.'[1]

More, however, takes place in the joining of Psalm 2 to Psalm 1 in order to create this introduction. Two critical directions are thereby given to the reader of the psalms that follow. One is the suggestion that we are to hear in the psalms the voice of the king, however subtly it may be present. The king's voice is only slightly evident in Psalm 2, in the prepositional phrase *'ēlay* of v. 7 and the divine direct address that follows it. The superscriptions of Book I, however, go on to make this direction quite explicit. There, and only there, are all the psalms placed on the lips of David.[2] The reader who encounters them now in this collection reads from Psalm 3 on as though one were hearing the voice of the ruler.

Completely apart from the point being made here, J.H. Eaton has proposed that some 21 of the 39 psalms in the first book of the Psalter are to be understood as psalms with royal content.[3] The proposal is not really surprising in light of the superscriptions following Psalm 2. The very first psalm the reader encounters, Psalm 3, is understood easily, if not preferably, as the voice of the king surrounded by his foes and praying for God's deliverance and blessing on the people or nation. But Psalms 4 and 5 also make sense as prayers of the king beset by enemies. In fact, one of the primary moves made in the hermeneutics of reading—created by adding Psalm 2 to Psalm 1 in the introduction—is a setting of the category of the wicked under the rubric of 'enemies'. The wicked are very present in Psalm 3, for

---

1.   Wilson, *Editing*, pp. 209-10. Wilson sees a larger editorial purpose at work in the placing of royal psalms at the seams between the books. His proposal has merit. What is being proposed here may be regarded as complementary to his analysis.

2.   As I have noted, the apparent exceptions in Psalms 10 and 33 are not really exceptions. They are to be read in connection with Psalms 9 and 32. Cf. Wilson, *Editing*, pp. 173-76.

3.   J.H. Eaton, *Kingship and the Psalms* (Sheffield: JSOT Press, 2nd edn, 1986). Even more radically, M. Bic has claimed to see in the whole of the first book of the Psalter, including Psalm 1, a liturgy for an enthronement festival in which the king plays a leading part. See M. Bic, 'Das erste Buch des Psalters: eine Thronbesteigungsfestliturgie', in *The Sacral Kingship* (*Numen*, Supp. 4; Leiden: Brill, 1959), pp. 316-32. (I owe the reference to Eaton's work.)

example, but they are there in the form of the enemies of the one who prays—David, the king. The enemies who oppose the anointed of the Lord are comparable to, and a part of, the wicked who oppose God's way as found in the Torah.

There is nothing that excludes or prohibits reading most of the psalms in the first half of Book I of the Psalter as coming from the mouth of the king. Out of Psalms 1–23, Eaton excludes only Psalms 6 and 12–15. Psalm 6 need not be excluded. It belongs to the sequence of prayers for help that begin the first book of the Psalter (Psalms 3–14). They become, by way of the reading encouraged upon us by Psalm 2, the vehicle of the ruler's plea for help against the nations and rulers that threaten, although it is not excluded that some of the enemies may be from within.

The only psalm that seems not to fit in this sequence of prayers is the hymn in Psalm 8, an apparent anomaly in an otherwise fairly consistent collection of laments. But its presence in this mix is to be accounted for on two grounds. One is the indication, even within this hymn, of the presence of the foes and the enemy who dominate the rest of these 'royal' prayers (v. 3). The other reason for including this particular psalm in the current position is an editorial one, unrelated to the general theme of lament or to the royal voice that can be heard in the prayers. As one sees in the editing/collecting of other psalms, the beginning and end of a psalm may provide a connection to the psalms, before and after, that accounts for its placement.[1] In this instance, the prayer of Psalm 7 ends with the vow of the king to 'sing

---

1. For example, the connection between Psalms 32 and 33 is in the way Psalm 33 begins as Psalm 32 ends. Cf. G. Wilson, *Editing*, p. 175, where he also notes that,

> Similar phraseology at the end and beginning of consecutive psalms is reminiscent of the Mesopotamian practice of providing successive tablets in a series with 'tag-lines' in the colophon which consisted of the incipit (opening line) of the next tablet in the sequence.

Psalm 43 is connected to Psalm 42 by the way its *final* line repeats the final line of 42. Psalms 103 and 104 belong together by virtue of their common use of *bārăkî napšî 'et-yhwh* at the beginning and end of each psalm. Psalm 107 at the beginning of Book V of the Psalter may be placed there because of the way it repeats the beginning of Psalm 106 and also answers the vow of v. 47—an editorial connection not unlike what we find in Psalms 7 and 8. The joining of several psalms by way of the rubric *hallĕlû-yāh* at the beginning and/or ending is, of course, obvious in the reading of Book V.

praise to the *name of the Lord*, O Most High' (*wa'ăzamměrâ šēm-yhwh 'elyôn*, v. 18). Psalm 8, then, is precisely such praise sung, as it opens with the words:

> O Lord [*yhwh*], our Lord, how majestic is your name [*šimkā*]
> in all the earth (v. 2).

The focus upon praise of the name is underscored by the repetition of this line at the end of the psalm (v. 10).

That verse, then, leads quite directly to the declaration or vow at the beginning of Psalm 9, which echoes 7.18 explicitly:

> I (will) give thanks to the Lord with my whole heart...
> I (will) sing praise to your name, O Most High (vv. 1-2)

The formulations at the end of 7.18 and at the end of 9.2 are exactly the same, including the reference to 'Most High' (*'elyôn*). The sentences are alike except that the *šēm-yhwh* of 7.18 becomes *šimkā* in 9.2, obviously echoing the repeated *šimkā* of 8.2, 10. Psalm 9.1-2 thus refers back to the praise rendered in Psalm 8 in accordance with the vow at the end of Psalm 7 and also continues to praise the name and recount the wonderful deeds of the Lord. Psalm 9 clearly sounds as if it is the voice of the ruler. The speaker praises God for rebuking the nations (v. 6) and judging the world and the peoples (v. 9) and claims the nations have sunk into the pit they have made for others (v. 16). The enemies are identified as the nations whose cities the Lord has rooted out (vv. 6-7). The nations, who are referred to five times in the psalm (the people are referred to twice), are also explicitly identified as 'the wicked' (*rěšā'îm*, v. 18; cf. *rāšā'* in v. 17). The fate predicted for them in Psalm 1 is the same as they are expected to suffer in 9.18.

One may properly understand the 'judgment' (*mišpāṭ*) upon the nations/wicked for forgetting God (9.16-21) as a reflection of Psalm 1 with its claim that the wicked cannot stand in the 'judgment' (*mišpāṭ*) because they do not live by the Torah. At least one major aspect of what it means to 'forget God' (v. 19) is to let go of the law or Torah that God has given to direct the human way.[1] Further, forgetting the 'needy' and the 'poor', for which the nations are judged, is itself an abandonment of the Torah and its frequent injunctions about the care of the needy and the poor. The care and protection of the poor and

---

1.   See Hosea, especially 4.6.

needy, the helpless, the afflicted, and the orphan—a theme that begins to take hold in Psalms 9–10 and continues on in the Psalter—is a major concern of the Torah or law of the Lord and an equally major responsibility of the king. The focus on the nations and the poor in Psalm 9 is picked up again in the explicitly royal Psalm 72 as the two major concerns of the king.

At this point, therefore, one recognizes a major link between Psalms 1 and 2 that is provided by Deuteronomy in its latest editorial stages. In the Deuteronomic law of the king, the ruler is given only one responsibility, one assignment. It is to have 'a copy of this law' (*mišnēh hattôrâ hazzō't*, Deut.17.18) with him always, to read in it all the days of his life, and to learn to fear the Lord by keeping all its words. In the Deuteronomic ideal of human rule, the *'îš* or 'one' whose delight is in the law of the Lord, and who meditates on it continually, is the king. The ideal ruler is thus the model Israelite.[1]

That means, however, that the way Psalms 1 and 2 introduce the Psalter, and especially Book I, is more complex than we have so far suggested. There is also a reverse way of reading from these psalms into the ones that follow than the one outlined above. The *dual* introduction creates a certain ambiguity for the reading of the psalms. The subject introduced to us is clearly the king against the enemies. But it is also the *'îš* against the wicked, that is, *anyone* who lives by the Torah of the Lord and thus belongs to the righteous innocent who cry out in these psalms. So one may not read these psalms as exclusively concerning rulers.

The anointed of God against the enemies and the righteous against the wicked may come together as the wicked become the enemies of the king and the ruler is the righteous sufferer before the wicked. But the king, indeed David, is a representative figure, and never more so than as the one who lives by the Lord's Torah. At that point, the ruler is the *'îš* of Psalm 1, but to no greater extent than any member of the community who delights in the law of the Lord and walks in the way of the righteous. Psalm 1 placed before Psalm 2, therefore, joins Deuteronomy in a kind of democratizing move that stands in tension with the royal one arising out of the placing of Psalm 2 as the lead into Psalms 3ff. While Psalm 2 invites the reader to hear the voice of the Lord's anointed in the following psalms, Psalm 1 says that what

1. See P.D. Miller, *Deuteronomy* (Interpretation; Louisville: John Knox, 1990), p. 149. Cf. Joshua 1.1-8.

we hear is the voice of *anyone* who lives by the Torah, which may and should include the king. But as such, the anointed one is simply a true Israelite even as he is a true king.

At this point, Psalm 8 comes back into the picture, contributing to the need to read the two subjects of Psalms 1 and 2 in lively tension with each other to the extent that they identify the voices and subjects of the psalms that follow them. For in Psalm 8, we encounter one of the clearest collections of royal motifs outside the explicitly royal psalms. But there, the royal figure is not a specific king or ruler:

> What is a human being (*'ĕnôš*) that you are mindful of such
> a one? (v. 5)

The answer the psalmist gives to the question posed is that *'ĕnôš*, the human being, wears a crown of glory and honor and exercises dominion and rule over all the creatures of the earth. The *'îš* of Psalm 1 is as much a ruler as the ruler of Psalm 2 is an *'îš*.

In such a complex but not obscure way, the first two psalms present the reader of this book with its subjects and especially those encountered in the first book of the Psalter. They are important clues that tell us many things about how to read without ever exhausting the possibilities. In various ways, as we have noted, their directions are congruent with other aspects of editorial shaping (for example the ascriptions of the psalms of Book I to David) as well as with possible historical critical judgments (for example the greater possibility of psalms in Book I being royal psalms).

BOOKS I–III AND THE EDITORIAL PURPOSE OF THE HEBREW PSALTER

J. Clinton McCann, Jr

In the past ten years, biblical scholars have given increasing attention to the shape and shaping of the book of Psalms. The investigation has proceeded on several fronts—investigation of how individual psalms may have been 're-read' or redacted to provide a 'new interpretation' for the postexilic community,[1] investigation of the links between adjacent psalms or among groups of psalms and investigation of the final form and editorial purpose of the entire Psalter.[2]

The most extensive work on the entire Psalter has been done by Gerald H. Wilson, who has proposed a new understanding of the editorial purpose of the Psalter.[3] After demonstrating that the fivefold division of the Psalter is intentional rather than coincidental, and after rejecting the attempts of Anton Arens and others to link the final form and editorial purpose of the Psalter to a three-year lectionary cycle, Wilson suggests that the purpose of the Psalter in its final form was to address the apparent failure of the Davidic covenant in light of the exile, the diaspora and the oppression of Israel by the nations in the postexilic era. The purpose of this paper is to support his proposal by presenting evidence which he did not cite, and by so doing, to add further depth and dimension to Wilson's conclusion.

---

1. See J. Becker, *Wege der Psalmenexegese* (SBS, 78; Stuttgart: Verlag Katholisches Bibelwerk, 1975), pp. 85-92; *Israel deutet seine Psalmen: Urform und Neuinterpretation in den Psalmen* (SBS, 18; Stuttgart: Verlag Katholisches Bibelwerk, 1966), pp. 41-68.

2. For an excellent summary of the recent research, see David M. Howard, Jr, 'Editorial Activity in the Psalter: A State-of-the Field Survey', *WW* 9.3 (Summer 1989), pp. 274-85, which is reprinted in this volume.

3. *The Editing of the Hebrew Psalter* (SBLDS, 76; Chico, CA: Scholars Press, 1985); see also the essays by Wilson in this volume.

Acknowledging the 'complex history of the composition of the Psalter' and the existence of smaller collections within the Psalter, Wilson proceeds, as other scholars have, on the assumption that editorial activity is most evident at the 'seams' between collections.[1] After examining Psalms 2, 41, 72 and 89, four psalms (three of which are royal psalms) at the 'seams' of Books I–III, Wilson suggests that Books I–III were arranged to document the failure of the Davidic covenant. Book I, a book of Davidic psalms bounded by Psalms 2 and 41, lays out the official theology. The king is God's son (Psalm 2) and can always depend on God's protection (Psalm 41, which is not a royal psalm but which, according to Wilson, 'echoes' the concerns of Psalm 2).[2] Book II, ending with a royal psalm attributed to Solomon (Psalm 72), has the effect of suggesting that the promise of God to David is good for Solomon and all other Davidic descendants as well. Book III, however, introduces a different note. At the end of Book III, Psalm 89 begins by rehearsing all the elements of the Davidic covenant (vv. 1-38), but it concludes that the covenant has failed (vv. 39-52). As Wilson concludes concerning Books I–III, 'The Davidic covenant introduced in Psalm 2 has come to nothing and the combination of three books concludes with the anguished cry of the Davidic descendants'.[3] The stage is now set for Books IV and V to answer the problem documented by Books I–III. Book IV, which Wilson calls the 'editorial heart' of the Psalter,[4] begins the answer by stressing that God is king and that God can be trusted in the present as God had been trusted in the ancient, Mosaic past before the Davidic monarchy ever existed. According to Wilson, Book V continues to address the dilemma of exile and dispersion by suggesting that deliverance is effected by trust in God alone (Psalm 107, which opens Book V), by obedience to God's law (Psalm 119, which, according to Wilson, dominates the central section of Book V), and by recognition of God as the only monarch worthy of human trust (Psalms 145–146, which represent the climax of Book V).[5]

Having briefly summarized Wilson's work, I now turn to my own.

---

1. Wilson, *Editing*, pp. 4-5; see p. 209. See also Wilson, 'The Use of Royal Psalms at the "Seams" of the Hebrew Psalter', *JSOT* 35 (1986), pp. 85-94.

2. *Editing*, p. 209.

3. *Editing*, p. 213.

4. *Editing*, p. 215; see pp. 214-19.

5. *Editing*, pp. 200-28.

As suggested above, I support Wilson's conclusion that the editorial purpose of the Psalter was to address the failure of the Davidic covenant in light of the exile and dispersion. I agree that Books IV and V provide an answer to the problem documented in Books I–III; however, my additional concern is to point out that Books I–III themselves *already* begin to answer the problem posed by the exile, dispersion and oppression of Israel by the nations in the postexilic era. Like Wilson, I shall focus on psalms at the 'seams' of Books I–III. In contrast to Wilson, however, I shall consider the psalms that begin Books I–III instead of concentrating principally upon the psalms that conclude these books. When one considers Psalm 1 as well as Psalm 2 at the beginning of Book I, Psalms 42–44 at the beginning of Book II, and Psalms 73–74 at the beginning of Book III, one discovers a pattern that serves to instruct the postexilic community not only to face the disorienting reality of exile but also to reach toward a reorientation beyond the traditional grounds for hope, that is, beyond the Davidic/Zion covenant theology. In attempting to support this assertion, I shall begin with Book III, because, as Wilson also recognizes, Book III most clearly reflects the failure of the Davidic covenant.

Book III

One can make several fundamental assertions about the nature of Book III. First, it begins with Psalm 73 which appears to be, and is usually interpreted as, a personal expression of someone who is in trouble but who is able at the same time to maintain hope. Furthermore, it is clear that this initial psalm of Book III is linked to subsequent psalms by the device of repetition. Psalms 73–83 form a Levitical collection, the Asaph psalms; and there are several instances of repetition that link Psalm 73 closely to Psalm 74 (see Table 1).[1]

---

1. See H.P. Nasuti, *Tradition History and the Psalms of Asaph* (SBLDS, 88; Atlanta: Scholars Press, 1988), pp. 63-66. Nasuti points out the literary links between Psalms 73 and 74, as well as links among Psalm 73 and several other Asaph Psalms. See also A. Caquot, 'Le Psaume LXXIII', *Sem* 21 (1971), p. 46; Caquot cites the literary links between Psalms 73 and 74 as evidence for relating them to the same chronological setting, which he proposes is shortly after the destruction of Jerusalem. See further Becker, *Wege*, pp. 116-17.

1)   superscription: *lĕ'āsāp*

2)   *miqdĕšê-'ēl*, 'sanctuaries of God', Ps. 73.17
        miqdāšekā, 'your sanctuary', Ps. 74.7

3)   *ḥāmās*, 'violence', in 73.6 and 74.20

4)   *yāmîn*, 'right hand', in 73.23 and 74.11

5)   *maššû'ôt*, 'ruins' or 'deceptions' in 73.18 and
        74.3 (the only two plural occurrences in the
        Hebrew Bible).

Table 1. *Literary links between Psalm 73 and Psalm 74*

Another fundamental assertion about Book III is that Psalms 74–83, all of which are linked to Psalm 73 by the designation *lĕ'āsāp*, are psalms of the community with the possible exception of Ps. 77.1-11.[1] As for the remainder of psalms in Book III, Psalms 84–89, four of the six are also psalms of the community. Only Psalms 86 and 88 appear to be psalms of the individual. In short, Book III of the Psalter is dominated by psalms of the community. A final, fundamental assertion about Book III is that most of the community laments in the Psalter appear in Book III. Among form critics, there is a consensus that Psalms 74, 79, 80 and 83 are community laments. In addition, many classify Psalm 89 as a community lament, and many either classify Psalms 82 and 85 as community laments or find motifs of the community lament in these two psalms. The community lament is clearly the dominant form or type of psalm in Book III of the Psalter.

These observations alone might be sufficient to establish the claim that Book III has been decisively shaped by the experience of exile and dispersion. An even closer examination of the canonical shape of Book III confirms this view. It is important to notice that except for Psalms 79 and 80, the community laments in Book III do not occur consecutively. Instead, they are interspersed with psalms which grasp for threads of hope amid the experience of exile and dispersion by celebrating God as judge of all the earth or by rehearsing God's past deeds on Israel's behalf despite Israel's faithlessness. Psalm 73, with its movement from lament to hope, sets the tone for the whole of Book

---

1.   See C. Westermann, *Praise and Lament in the Psalms* (trans. K.R. Crim and R.N. Soulen; Atlanta: John Knox, 1971), pp. 253-58. This portion of *Praise and Lament* was originally published as 'Zur Sammlung des Psalters', in *Forschung am Alten Testament* (Munich: Chr. Kaiser Verlag, 1965), pp. 336-43.

III. As Table 2 suggests, an examination of the final form of Book III reveals an alternation of expressions of lament and expressions of hope.

lament	Ps. 73.1-13	
hope	Ps. 73.18-28	
lament	Ps. 74	destruction of Jerusalem and rejection of Israel
hope	Ps. 75	God will judge the wicked (see vv. 3, 9, 11)
	Ps. 76	God will judge the princes and kings (see vv. 10, 13)
lament	Ps. 77.1-11	
hope	Ps. 77.12-21	God has led the people in the past
	Ps. 78	God's deeds on Israel's behalf despite Israel's faithlessness (see vv. 10, 17, 32, 40, 56); note the shepherd imagery and the root *nḥh* in the final verses of Pss. 77 and 78.
	Ps. 78.67-72	is a brief rehearsal of the Davidic/Zion theology
lament	Ps. 79	temple defiled and Jerusalem in ruins
	Ps. 80	plea for restoration (see vv. 4, 8, 20)
hope	Ps. 81	summons to praise and recalling past deliverance despite Israel's faithlessness
	Ps. 82	God has the power to judge all nations
lament	Ps. 83	the triumph of Israel's enemies (vv. 2-9) and plea for God's intervention
hope	Ps. 84	a song of Zion
lament	Ps. 85.1-8	plea for restoration
hope	Ps. 85.9-14	assurance of salvation
lament	Ps. 86	
hope	Ps. 87	a song of Zion
lament	Ps. 88	
hope	Ps. 89.1-38	a rehearsal of all elements of the traditional Davidic/Zion theology
lament	Ps. 89.39-52	rejection, defeat, destruction and plea for restoration

Table 2. *Alternation of expressions of lament and hope in Book III*

The effect of the final form is to suggest that Book III has been decisively shaped by the experience of exile and dispersion. The most direct reflection of the experience of exile is found, of course, in the community laments such as Psalms 74, 79, 80, 83, 85.1-8 and 89.39-52, which describe the destruction of Jerusalem and the temple, frankly confront rejection and defeat and plead for restoration. The experience of exile and dispersion, however, was not only a time for lamenting but also a time for forging new expressions of hope in an attempt to enable the community to survive. Thus, the psalms in Book III that celebrate God as judge over all the earth and all the nations should be understood against the background of exile and dispersion (see Psalms 75; 76; 81.12-17; 82) as should the psalms that rehearse the mighty deeds God had performed in the past despite Israel's faithlessness (see Psalms 77.12-21; 78; 81).[1] The two rehearsals of Davidic/Zion theology (Psalms 78.67-72; 89.1-38) and the two songs of Zion (Psalms 84 and 87) might be called two-edged expressions of hope. On the one hand, they serve to remind the community of God's past deeds on behalf of the people; on the other hand, the juxtaposition of traditional Davidic/Zion theology with laments of the community makes the traditional hope ring hollow at best.

The observation that the Asaph psalms, which form the bulk of Book III, are community-oriented and reflect the experience of exile and dispersion is not new.[2] What I am proposing builds on this observation but also moves beyond it; I propose that an analysis of the final

---

1.   See K.-J. Illman, *Thema und Tradition in den Asaf-Psalmen* (Meddelanden Fran Stiftelsens För Åbo Akademi Forskningsinstitut, 13; Åbo: Research Institute of the Åbo Akademi Foundation, 1976). In his study of the Asaph psalms, Illman points out that conflict (*Streit*) or punishment (*Strafe*) or judgment (*Gericht*) is a theme in every one of the Asaph psalms; but since judgment is sometimes directed at Israel and sometimes at the nations or enemies of Israel, Illman refuses to draw any general conclusion (p. 43; see pp. 30-38, 42). In my opinion, the interpretation of Book III against the background of exile and its aftermath explains why the judgment theme is variously directed. Judgment directed against Israel expresses the reality of exile and destruction, whereas judgment against the nations or enemies is a means of expressing hope. Illman also notes the use of historical rehearsal in several of the Asaph psalms (pp. 19-29, 42).

2.   See E. Beaucamps, *Le Psautier* (2 vols.; Paris: Gabalda, 1979), II, p. 4; J.H. Eaton, *Kingship and the Psalms* (London: SCM Press, 1976), p. 76; Illman, *Thema und Tradition*, pp. 55-64; A.F. Kirkpatrick, *The Book of Psalms* (Cambridge: Cambridge University Press, 1921), p. 430; see also pp. 427-29.

form of Book III reveals an arrangement that serves to assist the community not only to face squarely the disorienting reality of exile, as Wilson would suggest, but also to reach a reorientation based upon the rejection of the Davidic/Zion theology that had formerly been Judah's primary grounds for hope.[1] The canonical juxtaposition of the traditional Davidic/Zion theology with community psalms of lament serves to signal the rejection of this basis for hope. The juxtaposition is especially effective as one moves from Ps. 78.68-72, which rehearses the traditional theology, to Psalm 79, which begins by acknowledging that the temple has been defiled and Jerusalem destroyed:

> 78.68 but he chose the tribe of Judah,
> Mount Zion, which he loves.
> 69 He built his sanctuary like the high heavens,
> like the earth, which he has founded forever.
> 70 He chose David his servant,
> and took him from the sheepfolds;
> 71 ... to be the shepherd of Jacob his people,
> of Israel his inheritance.
> 72 With upright hand he tended them,
> and guided them with skilful hand.
> 79:1 O God, the heathen have come into thy inheritance;
> they have defiled thy holy temple;
> they have laid Jerusalem in ruins.
> 2 They have given the bodies of thy servants
> to the birds of the air for food,
> the flesh of thy saints to the beasts of the
> earth (RSV).

Psalm 89 also clearly suggests the need for reorientation that moves beyond the traditional Davidic/Zion theology, as Wilson pointed out.[2] After rehearsing every element of the traditional theology in vv. 1-38, the psalm makes an abrupt shift at v. 39, the effect of which is to call the preceding into question:

> 89.37 His line shall endure forever,
> his throne as long as the sun before me.
> 38 Like the moon it shall be established forever...

---

1. W. Brueggemann uses the terms 'disorientation' and 'reorientation' in his proposal for a modern typology of the Psalter; see 'Psalms and the Life of Faith: A Suggested Typology of Function', *JSOT* 17 (1980), pp. 5-6.
2. Wilson, *Editing*, pp. 212-14.

39 But now thou has cast off and rejected,
    thou art full of wrath against thy anointed (RSV).

Although the canonical shape of Book III points toward a rejection of the traditional basis for hope, it does not suggest an abandonment of hope; that is, it does more than simply document the failure of the Davidic covenant. As suggested above, the reach toward reorientation is represented by those psalms in Book III that look to God as judge of all the earth and that rehearse God's past deeds on Israel's behalf despite Israel's faithlessness. Furthermore, when the opening psalm of Book III, Psalm 73, is read in conjunction with Psalm 74 to which it is closely linked (see Table 1) and in the context of the Asaph collection and the rest of Book III, it too takes on a collective orientation.[1] The plight of the 'I' in Psalm 73 is to be understood in light of the exile and dispersion, and so the 'I' of Psalm 73 becomes an example to the postexilic community of how to respond to the problem of exile and dispersion. The final form of Book III instructs the postexilic community to respond to the failure of the traditional Davidic/Zion theology in the same way the 'I' of Psalm 73 responds to trouble:

26 My flesh and my heart may fail,
    but God is the strength of my heart
    and my portion forever (RSV).

In short, whereas Wilson is correct in asserting that the editorial purpose of the Psalter was to address the apparent failure of the Davidic covenant in light of the exile and dispersion, he does not go far enough. The answer to the problem is not limited to Books IV and V as he suggests; but rather the answer has already begun at least as early as Book III and perhaps earlier, as the following analysis of Books I and II will suggest.

Book II

The starting point in considering the shape of Book II of the Psalter is the observation that like Book III it opens with a Levitical collection,

---

1.   Compare my conclusion at this point with that of Illman, who describes Psalm 73 as idiosyncratic (*eigenartig*) among the Asaph psalms, because it focuses upon the destiny of the individual; see *Thema and Tradition*, p. 43; Nasuti, *Tradition History*, does recognize that Psalm 73 has a 'communal side', perhaps 'as a result of conscious adaptation' (p. 157).

Psalms 42–49, which are psalms attributed to the sons of Korah, and which, like the Asaph psalms, are generally oriented to the community. What is even more striking, however, is the similar pattern with which both books begin.[1] Like Psalm 73, Psalm 42–43 (which opens Book II and which I shall treat as one psalm) is presented as a personal expression of someone who is in trouble but who is able at the same time to maintain hope. In Psalm 42–43, the 'I' mourns the oppression of the enemy, while in Psalm 73 the 'I' is stricken and troubled by the prosperity of the wicked. In both cases, the enemies or the wicked raise questions about the psalmists' God. 'Where is your God?' they ask in Ps. 42.4, 11, while in Ps. 73.11 the questions are: 'How does God know? Is there knowledge in the Most High?'.

1.   superscription: *libnê-qōraḥ*

2.   the 'I' and the people face the 'enemy'; see *'ôyēb* in 42.10 and 44.17

3.   the enemy 'taunts' the 'I' and the people; see *ḥrp* in 42.11 and 44.14, 17

4.   the 'I' and the people suffer 'oppression' from the enemy; see *laḥaṣ* in 42.10, 43.2 and 44.25

5.   the 'I' and the people have been 'cast off'; see *zĕnaḥtānî* in 43.2 and *zānaḥtā wattaklîmēnû* in 44.10

6.   the 'I' and the people are 'forgotten' by God; see the forms of *škḥ* in 42.10 and 44.25

7.   the 'I' and the people are unable to see the 'face' of God; see *pĕnê 'ĕlōhîm* in 42.3 and *lāmmâ-pāneykā tastîr* in 44.25

8.   the 'soul' of the 'I' and the 'soul' of the people are suffering; see *napšî* in 42.6, 12 and 43.5 and *napšēnû* in 44.26

9.   the suffering is described with similar terms; 'my soul' is 'cast down' (from *šaḥaḥ*) in the refrain of Pss. 42–43 while 'our soul' is 'cast down to the dust' (from *šûḥ*) in 44.26

Table 3. *Literary links between Psalms 42–43 and Psalm 44*

1.   See M. Buss, 'The Psalms of Asaph and Korah', *JBL* 82 (1963), p. 383. Buss also notes this pattern, but does not consider it significant.

In both Books II and III, the opening psalm is followed by a community lament that is closely tied to the preceding psalm by several literary links. These links suggest in each case that the trouble of the 'I' and the expressions of hope in Psalms 42–43 and 73 are meant to be understood in light of the experiences of exile and dispersion that lie at the heart of Psalms 44 and 74 (Table 3).

The literary links between Psalms 42–43 and 44, as well as the fact that the phrase *libnê-qōraḥ* occurs in the superscriptions of Psalms 42–49, suggest at least that the Korah psalms should not be read in isolation from one another.[1] Thus, the royal psalm (Psalm 45), Zion songs (Psalms 46, 48) and the enthronement psalm (Psalm 47) that follow Psalms 42–44 should be heard in light of the experience of exile and dispersion. These psalms can continue to be expressions of hope and confidence; however, the expressions of hope become two-edged when they occur immediately following Psalms 42–44; that is to say, the traditional hope embodied in the royal psalms, Zion songs and enthronement songs is modified and reoriented by the literary context. In order to survive the crisis of exile and dispersion, Israel had to profess that God was, in some sense, still its 'refuge and strength' (Ps. 46.2), its 'secure height' (Ps. 46.8, 12; 48.4), and 'a great king over all the earth' (Ps. 47.3); however, such professions had to be understood differently when Israel spoke them no longer from the secure height of Zion but rather from a position of having been 'cast off' (Pss. 43.2; 44.10) and 'scattered...among the nations' (Ps. 44.12). The arrangement of the Korah psalms, in which Psalms 42–44 introduce Psalms 45–49, thus assisted the community to face the disorienting reality of exile and also to affirm that hope was still possible. The old words (Psalms 45–49) can still have meaning; but they must be heard in a new context—a context that includes an awareness of the reality of exile and dispersion (Psalms 42–44). When Psalm 42–43 is

---

1.   See G. Wanke, *Die Zionstheologie der Korachiten in ihrem traditions-geschichtlichen Zusammenhang* (BZAW, 97; Berlin: Töpelmann, 1966), pp. 1-39. Wanke's study of the Korah psalms is similar to that of Illman (*Thema und Tradition*) on the Asaph psalms. He concludes that the Korah psalms form a collection that is the product of the Korahite group or guild. Thus, Psalms 42–49 would reflect the same general historical or sociological setting as well as the same theological orientation. Wanke's view supports my conclusion that Psalms 42–49 should not be read in isolation from one another. See also M.D. Goulder, *The Psalms of the Son of Korah* (JSOTSup, 20; Sheffield: JSOT Press, 1982).

read in light of Psalm 44 and the rest of the Korah collection, it takes on a collective orientation. The refrain of the 'I' in Psalm 42–43 becomes an example for the postexilic community of how to face the problem of exile and dispersion:

> Why are you cast down, O my soul,
>   and why are you disquieted within me?
> Hope in God; for I shall again praise him,
>   my help and my God. (RSV)

Because the Korah psalms are community-oriented and because their arrangement reflects the experience of exile and dispersion, it is significant that these psalms serve as the opening collection of Book II of the Psalter. The Korah collection does not dominate Book II in the way that the Asaph collection dominates Book III, nor can one identify in Book II the alternation of expressions of hope and lament that is found in Book III. Nevertheless, the fact that Psalms 42–49 stand at the head of Book II, a redactional unit in the final form of the Psalter, suggests that Psalms 50–72 should also be heard in light of Psalms 42–49. In short, Psalms 42–44 thus provide a new context not only for reading the rest of the Korah collection but also for reading the rest of Book II. The canonical shape of Book II gives the reader a clue that the individual laments, which dominate the Davidic collection (Psalms 51–72), may legitimately be read not only as personal expressions of trouble but also as expressions of the plight of the community in the postexilic era. Like Book III, then, Book II is shaped to assist the community to face the disorienting experience of exile and dispersion and to reach a reorientation based upon a new understanding of the old grounds for hope. Again, in the way of adding another dimension to Wilson's conclusion about the editorial purpose of the Psalter, it appears that the attempt to answer the problem of exile and dispersion is not limited to Books IV and V but rather begins already in Books I–III.

Book I

As for Book I, we can be much more brief. At the beginning of Book I, Psalms 1 and 2 provide a literary context for reading Psalms 3–41 as well as for the Psalter as a whole. Just as Psalm 42–43 is linked to Psalm 44 at the opening of Book II and Psalm 73 is linked to Psalm 74 at the beginning of Book III, so Psalms 1 and 2 are linked by the occurrences of *'ašrê*, 'blessed' (1.1, 2.12); *derek*, 'way' (1.1, 6; 2.12); *'bd*, 'perish'

(1.6, 2.12) and *hgh*, 'meditate, plot' (1.2, 2.1).[1] Furthermore, Psalms 44 and 74 provide a collective illustration and general historical setting for understanding the problem that is stated in terms of the individual in Psalm 1, the problem of the wicked and the righteous. Although, unlike Psalms 44 and 74, Psalm 2 is a royal psalm rather than a community lament, it does deal with a problem that was pre-eminent in the exilic and postexilic eras—namely, the reality and continuing threat of the domination of Israel by the nations. By celebrating God as judge of the wicked (Ps. 1.4-6) and ruler of the nations (Psalm 2), Psalms 1 and 2 affirm the possibility of hope amid the realities presented by exile, dispersion and the loss of royal sovereignty and national autonomy in the postexilic era. By standing at the head of Book I, Psalms 1 and 2 also provide a literary context for reading Psalms 3–41. Thus, as in the case of Book II, the canonical shape of Book I provides a clue that the individual laments, which are predominant in Book I, may legitimately be read not only as personal expressions of trouble but also as expressions of the plight of the community. In short, the final form of Book I reveals a shape that is particularly suited for assisting the community to face the disorienting reality of foreign domination without a total loss of confidence, because the effect of the final form is to instruct the community to confront its crisis in the same manner as the 'I' of the individual lament, who is always able to face and express disorientation with an 'affirmation of confidence' or 'expression of certainty'.[2]

Conclusion

In summary, I maintain that the individual shapes of Books I–III of the Psalter support the view that the editorial purpose of the Psalter was to address the problem posed by exile and dispersion, namely, the apparent failure of the traditional Davidic/Zion covenant theology. An answer to the problem *does* come in Books IV and V, as Wilson suggests, but Books I–III already begin to provide answers. In adding

1. See J.P. Brennan, 'Psalms 1–8: Some Hidden Harmonies', *BTB* 10 (1980), p. 25.
2. See Gunkel, *Einleitung in die Psalmen: die Gattungen der religösen Lyrik Israels, zu ende geführt von Joachim Begrich* (Göttingen: Vandenhoeck & Ruprecht, 2nd edn, 1966), pp. 388-89. Gunkel uses the phrases 'affirmation of confidence' and 'expression of certainty' to describe a characteristic element of the individual lament.

another dimension to Wilson's work, I have taken into consideration the opening psalms of Books I–III (Psalm 1 as well as Psalm 2, Psalms 42–44, and Psalms 73–74), not just the closing psalms of these books as Wilson does. This has led to my conclusion that the final forms of Books I–III address the problem of exile and dispersion with the affirmation that hope is still possible, an affirmation that is particularly embodied in the opening psalms of each book:

> For the Lord knows the way of the
> righteous' (1.6), despite the conspiracy and
> plotting of the nations (Psalm 2).
> The people can still 'hope in God' and 'shall again praise'
> God (Psalms 42–43), despite being forgotten and 'cast
> off. . . forever' (Psalm 44).
> The people have God as their 'portion for ever' (Psalm 73),
> despite the destruction of Jerusalem and the temple
> (Psalm 74).

In assessing the value of Wilson's work and my own, the following points should be kept in mind. First, even if the new proposal for understanding the editorial purpose of the Psalter be judged as needing further elaboration and documentation, the proposal is valuable insofar as it leads to the consideration of the Psalter in a new light. As Joachim Becker has put it:

> What T. S. Eliot has said about Shakespeare applies to the Psalms: 'About anyone so great, it is probable that we can never be right; and if we can never be right, it is better from time to time we should change our way of being wrong'.[1]

Secondly, if Book III not only reflects the failure of the Davidic covenant (as Wilson suggests) but also begins to try to address the problem (as I am suggesting), then we may have a clue as to one of the groups involved in the editing of the Psalter. In his tradition-historical study of the Asaph psalms, Nasuti concludes: 'In the early postexilic era, the Asaphites were the only singers' group'.[2] In addition, he concludes that the Asaphites were involved in the liturgical life of the community, especially in ceremonies of communal lament; they were connected with cult prophecy and concerned with instructing, correcting and warning the community; and they were involved in 'theological

---

1. Becker, *Wege*, p. 9.
2. Nasuti, *Tradition History*, p. 187.

reflection on God's activity with respect to Zion'.[1] Given this set of involvements and concerns, and given that the Asaphites probably originated in the pre-exilic era and continued to exist well into the postexilic era, it is obvious that the exile would have been a major crisis for them. It also seems, however, that their involvements and concerns would have especially suited them to respond to the crisis of exile. Nasuti points out that the only major contradiction between the portrait of the Asaphites drawn from the Asaph psalms themselves and the Chronicler's portrayal of the Asaphites is that the Chronicler connects the Asaphites with praise and thanksgiving ceremonies rather than with communal lament ceremonies. Nasuti attributes this to the changed role of the group in a later historical period. He suggests that the praise psalms of the Asaphites did not make it into the Psalter along with Psalms 50, 73–83, because the Asaphite psalter 'was already closed'.[2] Is it possible, however, that the Asaphite psalter was compiled selectively for a purpose? Is it possible that Psalms 73–83 in particular were not collected randomly but were selected and arranged to address a crisis in the national life? Nasuti does not address the question of the purposeful arrangement of the Asaph psalms, but the portrait he draws of the Asaphites would make them prime candidates to address the crisis of exile; and it makes sense that they would do so by purposefully selecting and arranging their own primary sources.

Thirdly, if Wilson and I are correct or even if we are on the right track, our conclusion would mean that there is canonical warrant for understanding the final form of the Psalter as having a collective or corporate orientation; that is, it addresses the needs of a whole community. This conclusion would stand at odds, or better yet, in tension with the suggestion of Brevard Childs and others that certain features of the editing of the Psalter (for example, the superscriptions associating certain psalms with particular events in the life of David) focus attention upon the inner life of the psalmist and thus encourage individual appropriation by the faithful in any generation.[3] The tension

---

1.   Nasuti, *Tradition History*, p. 152; see pp. 120, 157-59, 188, 194-95.
2.   Nasuti, *Tradition History*, p. 190; see pp. 188-91.
3.   B.S. Childs, 'Reflections on the Modern Study of the Psalms', in F.M. Cross, W.E. Lemke and P.D. Miller, Jr (eds.), *Magnalia Dei, the Mighty Acts of God: Essays in Memory of G. Ernest Wright* (Garden City, NY: Doubleday, 1976), p. 384; *Introduction to the Old Testament as Scripture* (Philadelphia: Fortress Press, 1979), pp. 520-22.

between individual appropriation and orientation to a community is a fruitful one. While not denying that the psalms may address individuals in crisis in any generation, it also serves as a warning against allowing individual appropriation of the psalms to become a form of pious escapism that ignores the pain of others and the suffering of the world.

A CONTEXTUAL READING OF PSALMS 90–94

David M. Howard, Jr

The reading of the Bible as a literary work is commonplace today. On one level, a plethora of studies on individual texts has arisen that highlights many aspects of their literary qualities. On a higher level, many studies also are interested in the literary shapes of large corpora, including entire books and even larger collections (such as the Book of the Twelve).

The question of literary unity within the Psalter is a more complicated one than it is for most biblical books—owing to the discrete nature of each psalm and their early functions in liturgical settings—and it has been ignored for the most part in the history of Psalms study. In recent years, however, interest has turned precisely to this question of coherence within the Psalter, reviving an interest that had been present among scholars of an earlier time. The present volume is but one example of that.

I have reviewed elsewhere this concern with editorial activity in the Psalter, both on the higher level of the organization of the Psalter itself or of large collections therein and on the lower level of inter-psalm links.[1] The present essay will undertake to investigate the inter-psalm links of a group of consecutive psalms in Book IV, Psalms 90–94. Attention is paid primarily to lexical repetitions between psalms. The study is not exhaustive, in that it does not consider every lexical repetition among every psalm in this group,[2] but it considers the

---

1. D.M. Howard, Jr, 'Editorial Activity in the Psalter: A State-of-the-Field Survey', *WW* 9.3 (1989), pp. 274-85; reprinted (with additions) earlier in this volume.

2. For an example of the exhaustive method applied to eight psalms in Book IV, see my *The Structure of Psalms 93–100* (Ann Arbor, MI: University Microfilms, 1986). This study, along with the present essay, is part of a larger project on all of Book IV, which will consider every lexeme in all of its relationships, along with

significant links between adjacent psalms, as well as other links among non-adjacent psalms.

These five psalms do not form a meaningful unit in isolation, but they do exhibit interesting connections. Indeed, it would appear that we can see in Book IV a tripartite division, consisting of Psalms 90–94, 95–100, and 101–106.[1] There are overlapping links and echoes that jump across many psalms in Book IV, but these three groupings hang together especially well. Furthermore, within these groupings, Psalms 90–92 exhibit especially close links, as do Psalms 104–106. It would appear, then, that a concentric pattern of psalms exists in Book IV, centered on the core of the classic kingship of YHWH psalms.

This article examines the first of these groups. Particular attention is paid to the connections between Psalms 93 and 94, since the juncture between these two has posed problems for so many commentators.

1. *Introduction to Psalms 90–94*

Gerald Wilson's dissertation on the editorial processes behind the present Psalter was the first to highlight the major contours of the book—and the rationale behind them—in detail.[2] In it, he shows how royal psalms formed a backbone around which Books I–III were constructed. Concerning Book III, he focuses upon how it ends on an inconclusive note in Psalm 89.[3] The Davidic Covenant is strongly affirmed in the psalm (vv. 4-5, 20-38 [Eng. 3-4, 19-37]). However, that covenant is seen as being in the distant past (v. 20 [Eng. 19]: 'in days of old you spoke in a vision'; also, v. 50 [Eng. 49]: 'your tender mercies of old'), and, more importantly, as broken (vv. 39-46 [Eng. 38-45]). Note especially vv. 39-40 (Eng. 38-39):

> 39. But you: you have cast off and rejected, yes, you have been most angry with your anointed one. 40. You have renounced the covenant with your servant; you have defiled his crown in the dust.

As a result, the psalm ends with a classic lament form (vv. 47-52

---

other cohesive phenomena.

1. I am indebted to H.V.D. Parunak for triggering my thinking in this direction.

2. G.H. Wilson, *The Editing of the Hebrew Psalter* (SBLDS, 76; Chico, CA: Scholars Press, 1985).

3. Wilson, *Editing*, pp. 212-14. See further his second essay in the present volume, as well as the one by J.C. McCann.

[Eng. 46-51]; see, for example, v. 47 [Eng. 46]: 'How long, O YHWH? Will you hide yourself for ever? How long will your wrath burn like fire'). This lament asks deliverance from the present state of meaningless existence (see the root *šw'*, 'futility, vanity', v. 48 [Eng. 47]), and a restoration of YHWH's *ḥesed* of old (v. 50 [Eng. 49]).

We may note that the preceding psalm—Psalm 88—also contributes to the picture of disappointment at the end of Book III. This psalm is the bleakest of the laments, lacking as it does any clear expressions of trust in YHWH or vows to praise. Book III thus ends with a pair of psalms in which we find the psalmists doubting or questioning God.

In terms of the larger contours of the Psalter, the juncture between Psalms 89 and 90 forms a significant turning point, since the mood changes dramatically after Psalm 90. Wilson has noted this, as has Westermann.[1] Indeed, Westermann has noted that laments dominate the first half of the Psalter, while psalms of praise dominate the second, with Psalm 90 functioning as the pivotal psalm.[2]

2. *Psalm 90*

Psalm 90, as a psalm of Moses, is a reminder that YHWH's covenantal activity extended back not merely to David, but as far back as Moses. It begins by powerfully affirming YHWH's faithfulness as a refuge (*mā'ôn*, v. 1) and his eternal existence (v. 2).[3] This sounds a keynote for the powerful affirmations of his sovereignty that will be heard throughout Book IV.

The psalm speaks of the ephemerality of humans, however, in vv. 3-12, especially vis-à-vis the eternality of God mentioned in vv. 1-2. It does so in language reminiscent of the wisdom tradition. Portions of this section sound a cynical note—or, at the very least, one of weary resignation (see especially vv. 3, 5-7, 9-10)—such as that found in Ecclesiastes. The psalm ends with a lament form that calls for help in terms reminiscent of the lament at the end of Psalm 89.

---

1.   Wilson, *Editing*, pp. 214-15; C. Westermann, 'The Formation of the Psalter', in *Praise and Lament in the Psalms* (trans. K.R. Crim and R.N. Soulen; Atlanta: John Knox, 1981), p.257.

2.   Westermann, 'Formation', pp. 252, 257. We may add that the outline of the Psalter as a whole, then, mirrors the outline of the lament itself: both end with movements toward praise.

3.   On v. 2, see Ps. 93.2, which makes essentially the same point.

The psalm gives a few hints as to the answer to the problem of humanity's condition. Verse 8 mentions sins twice—'*wn*, 'iniquities'; '*lm* 'secret sins'.[1] Verses 7-12, and especially vv. 7-8, show that God's wrath is due to human sins. Thus, the problems that humans have are not so much due to God's unfaithfulness or whim, but to their sins. The key to the psalm—in terms of finding the psalmist's answer to the human problem—is found in v. 12: 'So teach us to number our days so that we might get a heart of wisdom'. In the context of the psalm, this indicates a positive attitude toward time, one that does not cynically or resignedly opt out of life, but that sincerely tries to account well for its days.

Psalm 90, then, serves as an effective bridge between the mixed message at the end of Book III and the towering affirmations in later parts of Book IV (and in almost all of Book V). It echoes the petition in the lament at the end of Psalm 89, and its weariness of spirit in vv. 3-12 echoes the questioning of YHWH in 89.39-46 [Eng. 38-45] and in Psalm 88. However, the psalm moves us forward, as well, to affirmations of YHWH. God is our eternal and faithful refuge (vv. 1-2). It tells us what Psalms 88 and 89 do not—that the poor human condition is due to sin (v. 8), and that the key to a well-lived life is to 'number our days', to aspire to wisdom (v. 12).

3. *Psalm 91*

Psalm 91 gives a much clearer answer to the human problem than Psalm 90 does, however. It echoes the idea of YHWH as refuge (see 90.1), specifically in 91.9 (*mā'ôn*, 'refuge'),[2] and in general throughout the entire psalm. It too has a decided wisdom flavor. This time it is of the didactic sort, where the psalmist instructs his listeners in the trustworthy ways of YHWH and the advisability of making God their security (vv. 3-13). The psalm ends with YHWH speaking (vv. 14-16), giving assurances of divine presence and protection. The keys to the relationship with YHWH are in loving God and in knowing God's name

---

1.   The occurrence of '*lm* here is a hapax in referring to sin; usually, its verb means 'to be hidden' (*niph*) or 'to hide, cover' (*hiph, hithp*).

2.   The word is used elsewhere in this way only at 71.3 (J. Reindl, 'Weisheitliche Bearbeitung von Psalmen: Ein Beitrag zum Verständnis der Sammlung des Psalter' [VTSup, 32; 1981], p. 351). Cf. the closely-related root *hsh* in vv. 2, 4, 9, meaning 'refuge, shelter', or 'to seek refuge'.

(that is, being in covenantal relationship with God; v. 14). Particularly striking is the affirmation about human longevity in v. 16a ('With long life I will satisfy him'), in light of the thoughts on the ephemerality of life that are expressed in Psalm 90 (especially vv. 4-6, 9-10).

4. *Psalm 92*

Psalm 92 is a psalm of thanksgiving. Read in conjunction with the preceding two psalms, it now expresses the reader's/worshiper's response to the assurances of Psalms 90 and 91, especially Psalm 91. It is full of the trust and thanksgiving that are largely absent in Psalm 90. It is the first psalm in Book IV that contains the classic vocabulary of musical and joyful praise (vv. 2-5 [Eng. 1-4]).

A specific key word linking Psalms 91 and 92 (by concatenation) is YHWH's *šēm* 'name' (91.14; 92.2 [Eng. 1]). Note also the reference to *'elyôn* 'Most High' (91.1 and 92.2 [Eng. 1]).

The psalm also echoes Psalm 90 in several ways. In Psalm 90, morning and night are terms used to emphasize human ephemerality (vv. 5-6); here, they symbolize the continuing praise of God for God's *ḥesed* and faithfulness (92.3 [Eng. 2]). YHWH's eternality also is emphasized in both psalms (90.2; 92.9 [Eng. 8]). A striking key-word repetition is *ṣûṣ*, 'flourish', in 90.6 and 92.8 (Eng. 7); in both cases it refers to the quick flourishing of the grass, which then quickly withers. In Psalm 92, the flourishing of the evil-doers is compared to the grass's in a trenchant and decisive analogy.

In general terms, Psalm 92 contains the answer to the petitions of Psalm 90, especially 90.13-17. Most strikingly, Ps. 90.14a asks YHWH to 'satisfy us in the morning (with) your steadfast love' (*śabbĕʿēnû babbōqer ḥasdekā*), while Ps. 92.3a (Eng. 2a) states that it is good 'to declare in the morning your steadfast love' (*lĕhaggîd babbōqer ḥasdekā*). Furthermore, 90.14b asks for these things 'that we may rejoice (*rnn*) and be glad (*śmḥ*) all our days', and 92.5 (Eng. 4) affirms that YHWH indeed has made the psalmist glad (*śmḥ*), and that he does rejoice (*rnn*).

And, finally, it should be noted that, like both Psalms 90 and 91, Psalm 92 contains a significant wisdom section, in vv. 6-10 (Eng. 5-9) (and also vv. 13-16 [Eng. 12-15]).[1]

---

1. Already in 1981, Reindl recognized the coherence of this unit of three psalms, focusing especially upon wisdom motifs ('Weisheitliche Bearbeitung', pp. 350-55).

5. *Psalm 93*

Psalm 93 introduces a string of kingship of YHWH psalms (93, 95–99). At first glance, there is little in Psalms 90-92 that is carried on in the following psalms; Psalms 92 and 93 have only five lexemes in common, and two of these are divine names.[1]

However, an important link is found in the connections of 92.9 (Eng. 8) and 93.2 and 93.4c, where YHWH's high position—a position that is eternal—is affirmed in all three verses.

> 92.9: But you, O YHWH, are on high [*mārôm*]
> forever [*lĕ'ōlām*]

> 93.2: Your throne is established from of old; you are
> from everlasting [*mē'ôlām*]

> 93.4c: Majestic in the heights [*mārôm*] is YHWH.

Another link is the occurrence in 92.6 and 93.5 of *m'd*, which is usually translated as 'very, exceedingly', but for which a case can be made that here it is actually 'O Mighty One', an epithet of YHWH.[2] Both psalms also affirm YHWH's house (*byt*) as a desirable place to be (92.14 [Eng. 13]; 93.5).

Psalm 93, and other psalms following Psalm 92, especially affirm YHWH's kingship, and the statement in 92.9 (Eng. 8)—'But you, O YHWH, are on high forever!'—serves to anticipate that well. In Psalm 92 this is not merely a minor statement that only rises to prominence in the light of its development in later psalms. It is a key motif and affirmation in Psalm 92 itself, and its use in following psalms confirms that. However, further confirmation of its importance within Psalm 92 is supplied in two ways. (1) Verse 9 (8) stands out as the only one-line verse in the psalm—or, better stated, the thought in the line that is verse 9 is succinctly stated, with no parallel thought to it, causing the line to stand out in bold relief in the psalm. (2) It stands at the exact midpoint of the psalm: a wordcount reveals exactly 52 words preceding it and following it. This 'centering' of a psalm's key point is

---

1. Indeed, Westermann echoed precisely this sentiment—he could find no connection between Psalms 90–92 and either Psalm 89 or Psalms 93–99 ('Formation', p. 255).

2. See Howard, *Structure*, pp. 47-48.

found in a fair number of psalms (for example, Psalms 8, 23, 95, 100).

Psalm 93 also affirms YHWH's eternality, and in doing so, it answers concerns raised in Psalm 90. YHWH's throne is from time immemorial (93.2), and God's decrees (and God's holiness?)[1] are forever (93.5). This psalm affirms YHWH's eternality in a confident way, not despairingly contrasting it with human ephemerality, as we find in Psalm 90. That YHWH is enthroned securely and eternally gives the faithful the confidence to face their own conditions and to ask God for help.

6. Psalm 94

Such a petition for help can be seen in the next psalm, Psalm 94. Psalm 94 is somewhat anomalous in terms of its position in the middle of a string of praise psalms, most of them affirming YHWH's kingship. It begins as a classic lament (vv. 1-7), and it refers only obliquely to the great kingship themes found in Psalms 93 or 95-99.

Despite this, however, there are more connections between Psalm 94 and its neighbors than are generally noticed. With reference to Psalm 93, these are relevant especially in the areas of common vocabulary and superscriptions.

a. *Psalms 93 and 94: Vocabulary*
A primary consideration in the editorial juxtaposition of any two psalms was significant vocabulary links.[2] Psalms 93 and 94 have relatively few lexemes in common, in part owing to their different subject matters and also to Psalm 93's relatively short length. They share eight lexemes, as follows:

> Group I:
> *g'wt* 'proud majesty' (93.1); *g'ym* 'proud ones' (94.2)
> *dky* 'pounding' (93.3); *dk'* 'to crush' (94.5)
>
> Group II:
> *nś'* 'to raise' (93.3; 94.2)
> *mwṭ* 'to waver, stagger' (93.1; 94.18)
> *ks'* 'throne' (93.2; 94.20)

---

1. So most versions; see Howard, *Structure*, p. 48, for a different reading.
2. See especially the works of Delitzsch, Alexander, Auffret, Brennan, Barth and Zimmerli mentioned in Howard, 'Editorial Activity', which appears earlier in this volume. Wilson's work pays little attention to this level, but these works tend to confirm his larger-scale analyses.

Group III:
ywm 'day' (93.5; 94.13)
rb 'many' (93.4; 94.19)
YHWH (93.1, 1, 3, 4, 5; 94.1, 3, 5, 11, 14, 17, 18, 22, 23)

Group III represents merely random or incidental repetitions. However, Groups I and II represent more significant repetitions; the most significant are in Group I. Each item in Groups I and II contributes to the picture of obvious contrasts between the psalms. What is significant here is that in each case it is YHWH—or YHWH's activity or attributes—that is contrasted with something or someone. In each case, an exact correspondence can be identified in the contrast.

The two paired roots in Group I provide the most significant keyword links.[1] The use of *gē'ût* (93.1) and *gē'îm* (94.2) is a case in point. In 93.1, YHWH's proud majesty (*gē'ût*)[2] stands in opposition to the rebellious waters of vv. 3-4. Juxtaposed against Psalm 94, it affords a vivid contrast to the proud, arrogant people (the *gē'îm*, 94.2) of that psalm. Throughout Psalm 94, what is at issue is human pride and arrogance; thus YHWH's pride in 93.1 forms the counterpoint to this in 94.2ff. The fact that YHWH is clothed with this proud majesty and with strength reduces the pride of the wicked ones of Psalm 94 to an insignificant or absurd position. In fact, the use of *gē'ût* in Psalm 93 contributes to the overall picture in that psalm of YHWH's strong position—as one who is powerful (v. 1), whose throne is secure (v. 2), and who is mightier than the waters. Confidence in YHWH's sovereignty provides a measure of justification for the call on God to intervene in the people's behalf in Psalm 94.

Another significant link between the psalms is found in the use of the roots *dky* (93.3) and *dk'* (94.5), meaning 'to crush, oppress'. Here, the sound of crushing by the rebellious waves directed against YHWH in Ps. 93.3 is of a piece with the oppressive crushing by the rebellious evil-doers directed against YHWH's people in Ps. 94.4-5. Both, in the final analysis, were rebellious attitudes or activities directed against

---

1. These two undoubtedly functioned as the main key words in any editorial decisions about juxtaposing the two psalms based upon vocabulary.
2. I translate *gē'ût* as 'proud majesty' in order to stress the continuity of the term's meaning with its cognates, which generally denote 'arrogance' in some form. The simple term 'majesty' (used by most versions in Ps. 93.1) is too bland.

YHWH. Anything or anyone that rebels against YHWH or crushes God's people is an enemy of both. Here again we can see that the confidence in YHWH expressed in Psalm 93—in this case, the fact that God was victorious and sovereign over God's enemies—forms the basis for the request in Psalm 94 that YHWH be assertive over the psalmist's enemies, and even for the confidence that God will do so.[1]

The roots in Group II, although less significant in functioning as key-word links, nevertheless contribute to the continuity in the way the two psalms draw contrasts. For example, on one level, the occurrence of *nś'* in both psalms is only incidental; in the one case (93.3), the reference is to angry waters lifting up a roar, and in the other (94.2), it is part of a plea for YHWH to act. However, there *is* some continuity here, since in Psalm 93 the roar is lifted up against YHWH, and in Psalm 94 YHWH lifts the divine self up against the enemies. Put another way, the roars of the waters arise in rebellion against YHWH in Psalm 93, and YHWH is called to arise in vengeance against God's enemies in Psalm 94. Furthermore, given the likely mythopoeic backdrop of Ps. 93.3-4—whereby the forces of nature were originally personified as gods—*nś'* can be seen in both psalms to be speaking of 'deity' asserting itself.

The use of the other two roots in this group, *mwṭ* and *ks'*, contrasts the stability associated with YHWH and the instability of the human condition. In 93.1, *mwṭ* (with *bl* 'no, not') refers to the unmovable condition of the world that YHWH has established, while in 94.18 it refers to the unstable condition of a human foot. In a similar manner, *ks'* speaks of YHWH's eternal and secure throne in 93.2, and speaks of an ephemeral throne of destruction in 94.20.

On the level of 'motifs' (that is, not strictly lexical repetitions), we may note the reference to YHWH's decrees in Psalm 93 (v. 5a) and YHWH's Torah in Psalm 94 (v. 12b). The word *'ēdōt/'ēdût* ('decrees, testimonies, warnings') occurs 32 times in the Hebrew Bible (25 of these are in the Psalter)[2] referring to the Torah. The echoes of the Sinai experience implicit in these terms are common throughout this section of the Psalter. In later periods, these terms came to be associated especially with the wisdom movement. Thus, both psalms refer to YHWH's words as communicated at Sinai.

---

1. See the excursus below for further evidence supporting the key-word status of the two lexemes in Group I.

2. Of which 21 occurences are in Psalm 119.

Excursus. The two sets of roots in Group I, *g'wt/g'ym* and *dky/dk'*, form the most direct contrasts between the psalms, and this accounts in large part for the special significance in their use. This significance is enhanced by consideration of where and how frequently they occur (although the argument above does not stand or fall solely on this basis).

gē'ût occurs eight times in the Hebrew Bible, three times in the Psalms.[1] *gē'eh* (pl., *gē'îm*) also occurs eight times, only twice in the Psalms.[2] Furthermore, the occurrences in 93.1 and 94.2 are the only ones in all of Book IV of either of these two roots or of any of the seven related roots.[3] Thus, of nine cognate terms—terms which occur 95 times in the Hebrew Bible, 14 times in the Psalms—the only two references in Book IV are these two in adjacent psalms—in 93.1 and 94.2. In fact, in only one other case in the entire Psalter do any of these roots appear in adjacent psalms, namely, *ga'ăwâ* (46.4) and *gā'ôn* (47.5).

This juxtaposition in adjacent psalms of a relatively common root, which is otherwise missing in Book IV, and which seldom is juxtaposed in any psalm pair, thus lends credence to the identification of the root as a key word in the two psalms.

There are four related roots associated with crushing/oppressing. (1) the verb *dk'* ('to oppress'), the most common of these, is found in Psalm 94; it occurs 18 times.[4] Its noun is *dakkā'*, which occurs 3 times.[5] (2) *dkh* ('to crush') occurs 5 times as a verb[6] and once as a noun.[7] (3) The adjective *dak* ('crushed, oppressed') occurs 4 times.[8] (4) *dŏkî* ('crushing'), the root in Psalm 93, occurs only once.[9] What is significant from these data is that of a total of 32 references, 15 of which occur in the Psalms, only three occur in Book IV.[10] Besides the two under consideration, the only other occurrence is at Ps. 90.3, where the reference is to dust, which is somewhat removed semantically from the term's main usage as 'crushing' and 'oppressing'.

Here, the juxtaposition of a somewhat rarer term, which is otherwise found only once in Book IV, and which likewise is seldom juxtaposed in any psalm pair, also favors its identification as a key word.

---

1.   Pss. 17.10; 89.10; 93.1; Isa. 9.17; 12.5; 26.10; 28.1, 3.
2.   Isa. 2.12; Jer. 48.29; Pss. 94.2; 140.6; Prov. 15.25; 16.19; Job 40.11, 12.
3.   *gē'* (1×), *ga'â* (5×), *gē'â* (1×), *ga'ăwâ* (19×), *gā'ôn* (49×), *ga'ăyôn* (1×), *gēwâ* (3×).
4.   Isa. 3.15; 19.10; 53.5, 10; 57.15; Jer. 44.10; Pss. 72.4; 89.11; 94.5; 143.3; Job 4.19; 5.4; 6.9; 19.2; 22.9; 34.25; Prov. 22.22; Lam. 3.34.
5.   It means 'crushed, contrite' in Ps. 34.19 and Isa. 57.15, and '[pulverized] dust' in Ps. 90.3.
6.   Pss. 10.10; 38.9; 44.20; 51.10, 19.
7.   Deut. 23.2.
8.   Pss. 9.10; 10.18; 74.21; Prov. 26.28.
9.   Ps. 93.3.
10.   These roots appear in adjacent psalms only one other time, but in what was originally one psalm: *dkh* (10.10) and *dk* (9.10; 10.18).

b. *Psalms 93 and 94: Superscriptions*

G. Wilson, in laying the framework for study of the editorial processes of the Psalter, has focused his attention in the book upon the psalm superscriptions, noting the significance of such things as groupings of titles of authorship and of genre.[1] As part of his study, he has treated the matter of untitled psalms—which includes Psalms 93 and 94—in some detail;[2] the patterns he has demonstrated have some significance for considering the editorial juxtaposition of these two psalms.

Wilson begins his discussion of the untitled psalms by noting that in Books I-III there is good evidence for seeing the juxtaposition of an untitled psalm with a preceding titled one as an editorial device to signal that psalm's association with the preceding psalm. In some cases— most notably Psalms 9–10 and 42–43—the second psalm was almost certainly originally a unified part of the preceding psalm.[3]

In several cases, however, what is noteworthy is that psalms which are almost universally judged to have been originally independent compositions appear now in the MT as 'pairs' in which the first is titled and the second is untitled.

In Book I, only Psalms 1, 2, 10 and 33 are untitled. Since the first two function as headings to the entire book, Psalms 10 and 33 stand out as the only two within Book I without titles (and, we should note, all the others are Davidic, as well). The case of Psalm 10 is clear: it is an acrostic with Psalm 9. Psalm 33, while probably not originally composed with Psalm 32, nevertheless exhibits numerous connections with the latter. Some manuscripts actually join the two, and the Old Greek's added title makes Psalm 33 Davidic.[4] Also notable is the fact

1.   By 'genre', Wilson means the ancient genres, such as *maśkîl*, *mă'ălôt* psalms, etc.

2.   Wilson, *Editing*, pp. 131-32, 135-36, 173-81; see also 'The Use of "Untitled" Psalms in the Hebrew Psalter', *ZAW* 97 (1985), pp. 404-13; and 'Evidence of Editorial Divisions in the Hebrew Psalter', *VT* 34 (1984), pp. 337-52.

3.   The absence of a title in Psalms 10 and 43—while Psalms 9 and 42 do carry titles—confirms this judgment, which is also made on other grounds. These include the broken acrostic across Psalms 9 and 10, and the repeated refrain across Psalms 42 and 43, along with the string of Korahite psalms from 42–49, as well as the unity of theme in both sets of psalms. Later manuscript evidence also supports this (Wilson, *Editing*, pp. 173-76; ' "Untitled" Psalms', pp. 405-407).

4.   On the special significance of titles of authorship for joining purposes, and the particularly disjunctive effect when strings of these end, see Wilson, 'Evidence of Editorial Divisions', p. 339; *Editing*, pp. 155-58.

that Psalm 33 begins as 32 ends. In 32.11, the righteous and upright in heart are exhorted to rejoice (*rnn*), be glad, and shout for joy in YHWH; in 33.1, similar encouragement of the righteous and upright in heart is present, including the exhortation to rejoice (*rnn*).[1]

In Books II and III, the only other completely untitled psalm, aside from Psalm 43, is Psalm 71. Here again various other lines of evidence combine to suggest the close connections between Psalms 70 and 71, including substantial manuscript evidence and the Old Greek's ascription of a Davidic title to Psalm 71, which Psalm 70 already has.[2]

In Books IV-V, the case of psalms with superscriptions is not so clear, since there are many more untitled psalms, many occurring consecutively. However, even here the convention seems to apply. Some manuscripts combine up to four consecutive psalms as one, and at least one combines five. Such large-scale combination occurs most frequently in two groupings: Psalms 90–99 and 114–119.[3] The presence of lengthy and complex compositions that emerge from such combinations argues against these having been composed together originally, but rather points to their combination having been an editorial one.

The longest unbroken stretch of untitled psalms in the Hebrew Psalter consists of Psalms 93–97.[4] Following the argument above, this points to a perceived unity among these on the part of the editors of the tradition underlying the MT.[5] While no one would dispute the

1.   On the other connections between the two, including the manuscript evidence, see Wilson *Editing*, pp. 174-76; ' "Untitled" Psalms', pp. 405-407. It is interesting to observe that Dahood noted both the lack of a superscription in Psalm 33 and the concatenation between the two psalms as editorially significant; these indicate 'that Ps. xxxiii is not a later addition and at the same time [explain] its lack of superscription' (M.J. Dahood, *Psalms I* [Garden City, NY: Doubleday, 1966], p. xxxi).

2.   Wilson, *Editing*, pp. 131-32, 177; '"Untitled" Psalms', p. 408. The apparatus in *BHS* is cognizant of the manuscript evidence, as well.

3.   Wilson, *Editing*, p. 177; ' "Untitled" Psalms', p. 409.

4.   See Wilson's Appendix C for a convenient tabulation of the superscriptions and postscripts for all the psalms (*Editing*, pp. 238-44). We should note that he includes phrases such as *hllw-yh* in his considerations; without these, the longest stretch of untitled psalms consists of Psalms 111–118, and Psalms 93–97 constitute the second-longest.

5.   Wilson takes pains in his discussion of Psalms 93–99 here (*Editing*, pp. 178-79; ' "Untitled" Psalms', pp. 410-11) not to overemphasize this point, especially in view of the nature of Psalms 94 and 95 vis-à-vis Psalms 93 and 96–99. However, the section, if it does anything, lends support to his argument rather than

unity of outlook among Psalms 93, 96 and 97, this fact about the lack of superscriptions urges a reconsideration of the usual judgments about the anomalous place of Psalm 94 (and Psalm 95) among the others. The presence of the formulaic YHWH *mlk* at the beginning of the group signals the initiation of a new composition here, after which the untitled psalms follow in succession. The absence of titles here indicates a dependence of sorts of each psalm upon the preceding one. (It even can be argued, on the basis of titles alone, that the stretch of unified psalms extends further, and consists of Psalms 93–99, although this does not materially affect the thesis here.)[1]

In the case of Psalms 93 and 94, then, there is a cohesiveness between them in the minds of the Psalter's editors, and the presence of the untitled Psalm 94 within a series of similarly untitled psalms must be seen as significant.[2] By subject matter, it is somewhat misplaced among a group largely composed of kingship of YHWH psalms. However, the lack of a title serves to 'soften' the disjunction, and to highlight its affinities with neighboring psalms, especially with its preceding psalm.

c. *Psalms 90–92 and 94*
When examined in the light of Psalms 90–92, the placement of Psalm 94 comes into even sharper focus. We have noted above that Psalms 90–92 form a group of psalms that shares a common wisdom vocabulary,

---

undercuts it, particularly since these two are more closely related to the others than is commonly supposed. (On Psalm 94's connections with Psalm 95 and following psalms, see Auffret, 'Essai sur la structure littéraire du Psaume 94', *Biblische Notizen* 24 [1984], pp. 69-72 and Howard, *Structure*, pp. 159-68, 206-207; for Psalm 95, see Howard, *Structure*, pp. 159-62, 168-76, 206-208.)

1.   The argument runs as follows. The only titled psalm among Psalms 93–99 is Psalm 98, simply called a *mizmôr*. Since 96.1 and 98.1 both contain the identical call to praise, *šyrw lyhwh šyr ḥdš*, a formula which recurs exactly in Ps. 149.1 and Isa. 42.10 (and cf. Pss. 33.3; 40.3; 144.9; Rev. 14.3), the presence of this title in Psalm 98 likely serves to emphasize the 'new start' (for a new song) mentioned within the psalm itself at this juncture. Thus, the presence of a simple title at Psalm 98 is only mildly disjunctive—it does not add any significant new information here, and it is not nearly as disruptive as would be a title of authorship (see p. 119, n. 1). The numerous connections Psalm 98 has with neighboring psalms (Howard, *Structure*, pp. 179-83, 194-96, 210-11) confirms the perceived unity among Psalms 93–99 indicated by their lack of titles. (The phrase beginning Psalms 97 and 99—YHWH *mlk*—also signals a 'new start' of sorts, although it too is not nearly as disruptive as would be a psalm title, especially of authorship.)

2.   Wilson does not consider the case of Psalm 94 in his discussions.

and they respond to each other in significant ways. Psalm 94 is linked
with these, as well, by virtue of its wisdom interlude in vv. 8-15.

This is especially true in the cases of Psalms 92 and 94. They share
20 lexemes, close to half of which are significant in one way or
another. Most of these are in the wisdom vocabulary found in both
psalms. For example, 92.6-10 (Eng. 5-9) speaks of the great gulf
between YHWH on high and God's enemies, who are spoken of—in
terms characteristic of wisdom—as dull, stupid, wicked, evil people;
these motifs are echoed in 94.4, 8–11. Again, Ps. 92.7 (Eng. 6) is
echoed in a remarkable way by 94.8:

> 92.7 (Eng. 6):
> The dull person (*ba'ar*) cannot know,
> the stupid (*kĕsîl*) cannot understand (bîn) this.
>
> 94.8:
> Understand (*bîn*), O dull ones (*ba'ar*) among the people!
> And, you stupid ones (*kĕsîl*), when will you become wise?

Also, the 'wicked' in 92.8 (Eng. 7) (*rĕšā'îm*) and the 'evil-doers' in
92.8, 10 (Eng. 7, 9) (*pō'ălê 'āwen*) are prominent in Psalm 94, as well
—the *rĕšā'îm* are seen in 94.3, 3, 13, and the *pō'ălê 'āwen* in 94.4, 16.

Both psalms (92 and 94) show the wicked and the foolish who may
flourish for a moment, but who will ultimately be overcome by
YHWH and YHWH's righteousness; YHWH intercedes on behalf of
YHWH's own righteous people. As Marvin Tate notes,

> Ps. 94 summons those with weak faith and lax commitment to a renewed
> perception of the work of Yahweh which would permit them to join in the
> acclamation of his kingship. At the same time, both psalms...serve as a
> rebuke and warning to the wicked...[1]

Psalm 94 comes full circle in the first section of Book IV by echoing
Psalm 90 in several ways, as well. The lament/petition in Psalm 90
comes at the end of that psalm (90.13-17), leaving one with a sense of
irresolution. In Psalm 94, the lament/petition comes at the beginning
(94.1-7), but it is followed by sustained expressions of trust in YHWH,
which are in accordance with the trust expressed in all the kingship of
YHWH psalms surrounding it. These are the only two psalms in Book
IV that contain a lament portion until Psalm 102.

---

1. M.E. Tate, *Psalms 51–100* (WBC, 20; Waco: Word Books, 1990), p. 488.
(I am indebted to Professor Tate for placing portions of his manuscript at my
disposal prior to publication.)

Lexically, Psalms 90 and 94 have 21 roots in common. Most are incidental repetitions, but three of significance can be noted. (1) In 90.2 and 94.2, YHWH is noted as sovereign over the earth (*'rṣ*), as creator and as judge, respectively. (2) In both psalms, the ability to know (*yd'*) is important; in 90.11, no human can know the power of YHWH's anger, while in 94.11, on the other hand, YHWH knows the very thoughts of humans. (3) The heart (*lbb*) is the seat of right living and desires; in 90.12, a heart of wisdom is to be desired, while in 94.15, the upright of heart are commended.

Both psalms emphasize the motif of the ephemerality of life (90.5-6, 9-10; 94.11). The latter psalm, however, speaks of it more positively, in a context of YHWH's benign sovereignty.

d. *Psalm 94 among the Kingship of* YHWH *Psalms*

In light of the above considerations, the placement of Psalm 94 should no longer be seriously questioned. However, in addition to these, two further points can be made in assessing its placement here, specifically as it relates to the motifs of YHWH's kingship. First, in 94.1, YHWH is seen as the God of 'vengeance' (*nqmwt*). George Mendenhall has pointed out that the function of this 'vengeance' is a royal one, a function of a king or of YHWH, in their exercise of legitimate executive power.[1] Thus, Psalm 94, in calling forth the exercise of YHWH's avenging power, indeed recognizes YHWH's royal authority, and easily assumes its place among the kingship of YHWH psalms.[2]

Secondly, Ps. 94.1-2 is a call for a theophany, for YHWH to appear and act. Watts has pointed out that one feature of the kingship of YHWH psalms is 'words showing characteristic acts of Yahweh, including creating, making, establishing, sitting, doing wonders, judging, doing righteous acts and saving'.[3] In this respect, too, then, Psalm 94 fits well with these kingship psalms.

---

1. G.E. Mendenhall, 'The "Vengeance" of Yahweh', in his *The Tenth Generation* (Baltimore: Johns Hopkins University Press, 1973), pp. 70-104.

2. Tate, *Psalms 51–100*, pp. 489-90.

3. J.D.W. Watts, 'Yahweh *Mālak* Psalms', *TZ* 21 (1965), pp. 341-48.

7. Conclusion

Significant links can be seen between every consecutive psalm in Psalms 90–94, and between many non-adjacent psalms as well. The coherence among these five psalms is suggestive of the same phenomenon in the next grouping in Book IV—Psalms 95–100. Psalms 95 and 100 especially relate to each other (see especially 95.6-7 and 100.3).[1] It may well be, then, that the structure of Book IV is dependent upon the series of three groups mentioned above—90–94, 95–100, and 101–106—each with a relative internal coherence and significant subgroupings within it, and each also relating in significant ways to the others. However, that is the subject of another treatment.[2]

1. See Howard, *Structure*, pp. 78, 134, 174-76, 207-208.
2. See above, p. 108 n. 2.

INDEXES

INDEX OF REFERENCES

OLD TESTAMENT

JOURNAL FOR THE STUDY OF THE OLD TESTAMENT

Supplement Series